THE OLD TESTAMENT: AN INTRODUCTION
Volume 2
Prophetic Traditions

THE OLD TESTAMENT: AN INTRODUCTION

Volume 2
Prophetic Traditions

Paul Nadim Tarazi

ST VLADIMIR'S SEMINARY PRESS
Crestwood, New York, 10707-1699
1994

Library of Congress Cataloging-in-Publication Data
Tarazi, Paul Nadim, 1943-
    The Old Testament.

    Includes bibliograpical references and indexes.
    Contents: v. 1. Historical traditions—v. 2. Prophetic traditions.
    1. Bible. O. T.—Introductions. I. Title.
BS1140.2.T27   1991   221.6'1   91-26542
ISBN 0-88141-105-1 (v. 1)
ISBN 0-88141-106-X (v. 2)

Copyright © 1994, Paul Nadim Tarazi

ISBN 0-88141-106-X

To Georges Khodr
Metropolitan of Byblos and Mount Lebanon
in everlasting gratitude
for the late 1950's and early 1960's

Volume Table of Contents

Table of Contents

II — The Pre-Exilic Period

III — The Exilic Period

IV — The Post-Exilic Period

Summary Chronology of the Prophets

Kingdom of Israel	922-722/21 B.C.
Jeroboam II	783-743
Amos	750
Hosea	750-743
Fall of Samaria	722/21
Kingdom of Judah	922-587 B.C.
Isaiah	740-700
Micah	740-730
Jeremiah	627-580
Nahum	625 or 612
Zephaniah	620
Habakkuk	620-610
Fall of Jerusalem	587
Babylonian Exile	597/587-537 B.C.
Ezekiel	597-570
Second Isaiah	545-538
Persian Period	538-331 B.C.
Haggai and Zechariah	520-518
Joel, Obadiah, and Jonah	5th-4th centuries
Third Isaiah	4th century
Second Zechariah and Malachi	4th century
Hellenistic Period	331-63 B.C.
Daniel	167-164

Abbreviations

Books of the Old Testament*

Gen	Genesis	Job	Job	Hab	Habakkuk
Ex	Exodus	Ps	Psalms	Zeph	Zephaniah
Lev	Leviticus	Prov	Proverbs	Hag	Haggai
Num	Numbers	Eccl	Ecclesiastes	Zech	Zechariah
Deut	Deuteronomy	Song	Song of Solomon	Mal	Malachi
Josh	Joshua	Is	Isaiah	Tob	Tobit
Judg	Judges	Jer	Jeremiah	Jdt	Judith
Ruth	Ruth	Lam	Lamentations	Wis	Wisdom
1 Sam	1 Samuel	Ezek	Ezekiel	Sir Sirach	(Ecclesiasticus)
2 Sam	2 Samuel	Dan	Daniel	Bar	Baruch
1 Kg	1 Kings	Hos	Hosea	1 Esd	1 Esdras
2 Kg	2 Kings	Joel	Joel	2 Esd	2 Esdras
1 Chr	1 Chronicles	Am	Amos	1 Macc	1 Maccabees
2 Chr	2 Chronicles	Ob	Obadiah	2 Macc	2 Maccabees
Ezra	Ezra	Jon	Jonah	3 Macc	3 Maccabees
Neh	Nehemiah	Mic	Micah	4 Macc	4 Maccabees
Esth	Esther	Nah	Nahum		

Books of the New Testament

Mt	Matthew	Eph	Ephesians	Heb	Hebrews
Mk	Mark	Phil	Philippians	Jas	James
Lk	Luke	Col	Colossians	1 Pet	1 Peter
Jn	John	1 Thess	1 Thessalonians	2 Pet	2 Peter
Acts	Acts of the Apostles	2 Thess	2 Thessalonians	1 Jn	1 John
Rom	Romans	1 Tim	1 Timothy	2 Jn	2 John
1 Cor	1 Corinthians	2 Tim	2 Timothy	3 Jn	3 John
2 Cor	2 Corinthians	Titus	Titus	Jude	Jude
Gal	Galatians	Philem	Philemon	Rev	Revelation

*Following the larger canon known as the Septuagint.

Foreword

This is the second book in a trilogy of introductions to the literature of the Old Testament. Like the first volume, this one is divided into four parts. In part one I venture an exegesis of the book of Amos in order to show how one can discern the original words of the prophet himself, the words of later editors, and the text's intended message. My choice of Amos as a prototype worth focusing on stems from the following considerations: (a) Amos is chronologically the first among the prophets whose names are ascribed to books; (b) his teachings reflect virtually all the essential points common to the "prophetic message" as discussed in the Introduction; and (c) the size of the book makes a comprehensive study manageable.

Parts two, three, and four examine the rest of the prophets and divide them into three periods: pre-exilic, exilic, and post-exilic. The goal here is to cover what I consider to be the specific input of each of the subsequent prophets, thereby sparing the reader the tediousness of going time and again over elements common to more than one prophet. And on the positive side, discussing in more detail the particular contribution of each prophet will help illuminate the lengthy and, at times, meandering path of God's "prophetic word" over the centuries. My hope is that such an endeavor will help the reader to see this prophetic word "at work."

This volume would not have seen the light in its present form were it not for the extensive input of Tom Dykstra, a former student of mine and a very close colleague since his graduation from seminary. Whatever clarity and pointedness the text may display are due to his ability to correctly comprehend my arguments, his mastery of English, and his rephrasing of my words into language more accessible to the common reader. To that end he enlisted the unselfish help of his mother, Wilma Dykstra; also well versed in English but lacking a seminary education, she reviewed the text from a "layman's" perspective and offered valuable suggestions for improving it. Mr. Dykstra's tedious work of editing this book included verifying the biblical references and the wording of the scriptural quotations. My indebtedness to him is beyond words as, I hope, will be the reader's gratitude. Needless to say, however, I bear the sole responsibility for any weakness or inadequacy in the content of the present work as well as for whatever difficulty it may cause the reader.

Paul Nadim Tarazi

Introduction*

There are words which through overuse have become so loaded with different connotations that an author cannot simply assume his readers will understand what he means by them. "Prophet" is such a word. No longer limited to the theological field, today it is so fashionable that nearly everyone uses it: in religious circles, in politics, in literature, in science, etc. But can it always carry precisely the same meaning in such widely varying contexts? Not likely. In fact, even within the theological field people have differing views as to what constitutes prophetism. Therefore, one must begin a study of the biblical prophets by determining just what is meant by "prophet" in the biblical context.

To do that it will be necessary to compare and contrast the biblical prophet with other classes of individuals. In other words, I will not begin with the assumption—popular in some circles—that the biblical prophet is an absolutely unique individual and biblical prophetism an absolutely unique phenomenon. Such an assertion would contradict our Orthodox Christian faith. We believe that only God is absolutely unique in his trinitarian oneness and does not fit into any category by which he could be compared with anyone or anything else. For that reason our tradition has reserved the name *theologia* ("theology" in the strictest sense) for this area of religious interest and has advised silence as the best approach to it. Because no comparison is possible, no description or definition is possible. That being the case, even if

* An earlier version previously published in *God's Living Word: Orthodox and Evangelical Essays on Preaching,* Brookline, MA, Holy Cross Orthodox Press, 1983.

we dared to argue that the prophets were really unique in the absolute sense we attribute to God, we would come up against our tradition's admonishment to be silent in the face of such incomparability. Besides, any study of the prophets would be of little practical value to anyone if the prophets, due to their absolute uniqueness, could not be considered examples for us today to emulate.

So whatever uniqueness the biblical prophets do possess must be relative or limited, and the study of them belongs not to the silent realm of *theologia* but rather to *oikonomia* ("economy" —God's activity in the world) where comparison and description are not only permitted but are useful and even necessary. Consequently, we will proceed to discover what did indeed set the prophets apart, by categorizing them as a group of individuals and viewing them against the background of other similar and dissimilar groups which the biblical texts tell us about.

The Prophets as Public Speakers

Any reader of the Bible cannot help but notice that the Old Testament prophets appeared on the historical scene as public speakers. This obvious fact, then, ought to be the starting point in our research. Now in this broad category of what we call public speakers we find in ancient Israel three main sub-categories: the priests, the elders or wise men, and the seers. Let us have a quick glance at the characteristics of each.

The priests administered the public religious life either of a central temple or a local shrine. Both biblical and extra-biblical literature provide abundant evidence that one main aspect of their cultic duties was to address the people who came to worship at God's altars. In fact, people would visit those altars not only for the purpose of offering sacrifices, but also to seek divine guidance at the places where God himself had appeared to their forefathers, where his presence could still be felt and his voice heard. It is no coincidence that altars tended to be located at the precise spots where God had once manifested himself. The divine message created the holy place, and men sought it out afterwards mainly to seek God's instruction. If we may characterize the sacrifices they offered there as man's offering to God or man's part in the encounter between the two, then the *torah* (instruction) delivered by the priest was God's "offering" to man, God's part in that same encounter.

Constituting the second important category of public speakers are the wise men or elders. Wisdom is usually related to age because it is based on personally experienced knowledge, as opposed to academic learning which a person of any age can get from books. We customarily associate the activity of the wise men with the proverbs found in many an Old Testament book. These proverbs were the end result of a long process which took place at the town gates or market places. It was to those "meeting places of human minds" that people came to seek help, guidance, wisdom, and solutions to their problems. The answers came from noted elders and wise men, forerunners of the philosophers. As with the priest, the message propounded by the elder was central to the meeting, its very purpose—and a civilization which believed "the fear of the Lord is the beginning of knowledge" (Prov 1:7) must have seen in that message a reflection of God's own wisdom.

Last but not least there are the seers. While one would consult a priest or an elder either on a regular basis or for a specific purpose, one would approach the seer only for the latter reason, i.e., to get an answer or clarification regarding a particular issue or question. The fact that the issue or question could involve a large group of people—even the entire nation—and the fact that the seer would be expected to provide the solution almost instantaneously, created a special halo around him, making of him the "man of God" par excellence. In his presence people felt more than with anyone else the immediacy of God himself.

Though brief, this survey shows that the uniqueness of the biblical prophet which would differentiate him from one of these other kinds of public speaker is not immediately obvious. Nothing either in content or in form differentiates a priori the message of the prophet from that of the other public speakers—all were holders and purveyors of God's word. The prophets sounded at times like the priests whose authority was based on a *torah* (a fixed, written set of instructions) and at times like the elder and the seer who spoke on their own authority. The prophet shared with the priest a preference for delivering his message in the vicinity of an altar,[1] and in fact some of the prophets were actually priests themselves. But on the other hand, biblical research has also shown that both the content and form of many prophets' proclamations were influenced by the so-called "wisdom literature." Finally, what I said concerning the immediacy of God felt in the seer's utterances could be applied with equal validity to the prophet, as can be seen from the fact that the Israelite and Judahite traditions bestowed the same word *nabi'* on both the prophets and the seers.

The Aggressiveness of God

What is it then that makes the prophetic word unique or at least differentiates it from the word of the priest, the elder, or the seer? In a word, that special quality is God's *aggressiveness*. Let me immediately explain what I mean by that term in this context. Yahweh had formed Israel in the exodus from Egypt and from that beginning made it grow into a nation. But if an enslaved people could become a nation, the nation could also become again an enslaved people. Only he who created the nation could preserve the nation from disintegration. So Israel's only hope for survival was to continue to seek Yahweh's counsel through the officially appointed channels—the priests, the elders, and to a certain extent the seers. The Lord was present in his instruction

---

1. I believe the reason for that is not so much practical (an altar would be a convenient place to find an audience) as it is theological: at the altar one speaks on God's behalf.

(*torah*) at the altars and in his wisdom at the city gates; he was even accessible in an immediate way through the "men of God" (the seers) for special requests. However, notice that in all these cases the public speakers were usually sought and consulted; they did not take the initiative themselves. It was the people who took the initiative to go and ask for guidance. In other words, God responded when queried.

All was fine until something went wrong. And what went wrong was neither the priesthood nor the institution of wisdom nor the seers. No! What went wrong was the mentality of God's people: they decided they were the center of the universe, the masters of their own destiny. Once Israel and Judah were firmly established in their lands by Yahweh, nothing was left for the Mighty Redeemer to do except settle in his lofty throne, relax, enjoy the results of his great deed, and perhaps use his great wisdom to help solve some domestic disputes whenever consulted. Thus thought Israel.

Suddenly God's behavior changed radically, or so it seemed to his people: the Lord started questioning instead of answering; he triggered the conversation; he opened the discussion; he took the initiative. And he chose the place of encounter instead of leaving it to the people. They used to come to him at his altars and the city gates, veiling their sins under a pretense of piety. Now he went out to meet them in their homes, in the streets, and at their workshops, unveiling their sinful hearts. But, they objected, he can't do this—he is breaking all the rules of conventional behavior, the rules he himself originally set. The rules were not designed to fetter him, he replied, and he broke them all. Why? Well, an unconventional approach needed an unconventional solution: not the priests, he said, nor the elders, nor the seers, but the unknown whose lips God would choose to purify and make resound with his own words. In a word, the Lord became "aggressive."

This aggressiveness is felt already at the formal level of the prophetic words. Expressions like "Oracle of the Lord," "Word of the Lord," and "Thus says the Lord," not only abound in the prophetic writings, but are characteristic of them. One ought to include also the editorial expression, "The Word of the Lord came to so and so." These all clearly reflect the prophets' consciousness that God was not underlining some points of a predefined and set-in-concrete *torah*, nor was he just giving another word of wisdom, nor was he speaking in response to someone's query as to a seer. Rather, he was initiating the conversation; he was addressing the people with the creative power of his word as he had done on the day he created Israel and Judah; he was making a completely new move; he was launching a new era in his activity; he was coming up with something which "no one has heard or perceived by the ear, no eye has seen" (Is 64:4). If this is true—and when it canonized the prophetic writings, our church agreed that it is—then the prophetic word is authoritative, its content normative, and its study necessary for any serious effort to know God. So without further ado, let us get started in that effort by looking at some typical aspects of the prophetic message.

The Coming End

The prophetic message is essentially one of discontinuity, a break with the past. But for God, breaking with the past means undoing or reversing the past. If he is the Creator, Redeemer, and Lord of Israel and Judah, then his breaking away from his people would mean the breaking up of that community itself. The unconventional messenger of God brought along the unconventional message of a total end: the end of God's people Israel and/or Judah. And nothing could be of any help in averting that end—not any mighty earthly nation or power, not even the holy temple of Yahweh itself. Let us listen to some prophetic voices:

"... yet you did not return to me," says the Lord. "Therefore thus I will do to you, O Israel; because I will do this to you, prepare to meet your God,

O Israel!" (Am 4:11-12)

Therefore thus says the Lord: "Your wife shall be a harlot in the city, and your sons and your daughters shall fall by the sword, and your land shall be parceled out by line; you yourself shall die in an unclean land, and Israel shall surely go into exile away from its land." (Am 7:17)

Then the Lord said to me, "The end has come upon my people Israel; I will never again pass by them." (Am 8:2)

Woe to those who go down to Egypt for help and rely on horses, who trust in chariots because they are many and in horsemen because they are very strong, but do not look to the Holy One of Israel or consult the Lord! And yet he is wise and brings disaster, he does not call back his words, but will arise against the house of the evildoers and against the helpers of those who work iniquity. The Egyptians are men, and not God; and their horses are flesh, and not spirit. When the Lord stretches out his hand, the helper will stumble, and he who is helped will fall, and they will all perish together. (Is 31:1-3; cf. 30:1-7)

The word that came to Jeremiah from the Lord: "...Do not trust in these deceptive words: 'This is the temple of the Lord, the temple of the Lord, the temple of the Lord!'... Go now to my place that was in Shiloh, where I made my name dwell at first, and see what I did to it for the wickedness of my people Israel. And now, because you have done all these things, says the Lord, and when I spoke to you persistently you did not listen, and when I called you, you did not answer, therefore I will do to the house which is called by my name, and in which you trust, and to the place which I gave to you and to your fathers, as I did to Shiloh. And I will cast you out of my sight, as I cast out all your kinsmen, all the offspring of Ephraim." (Jer 7:1, 4, 12-15)

"End" may not always mean "annihilation"; the latter is only one form, aspect, or expression of the former. That is why we may view the post-exilic prophecies of restoration as also carrying the message of an end—the end of a despairing Judah which had lost hope in its God because the situation seemed hopeless; the end of a Judah which took its own senses more seriously than it did God; the end of a Judah which forgot that God is the Lord of all situations, good and bad alike. These too are proclamations of an "end":

Comfort, comfort my people, says your God. Speak tenderly to Jerusalem, and cry to her that her warfare is ended, that her iniquity is pardoned, that she has received from the Lord's hand double for all her sins. (Is 40:1-2)

For behold, I create new heavens and a new earth; and the former things shall not be remembered or come into mind. (Is 65:17)

All of this points in one direction: every time there were signs that people were beginning to behave as if God were no longer their Lord, he put an end to that situation, smashing the false image they had erected of him. God is God and intends to remain so. Whenever Israel or Judah boasted in their richness and earthly accomplishments, disregarding God's instructions, the Lord came with his mighty hand to strike his own nation down, and whenever Judah was on the verge of losing faith and hope in him, the same God intervened with the same mighty hand to work wonders in its favor.

God Himself Causes the End

The "end" in the prophetic understanding is not a natural phenomenon in the sense that everything has, after all, a final chapter—good fortune as well as misfortune, greatness as well as debasement, etc. For the prophet, it is not a question of things happening because they are at the end of their cycle and their time, as it were, has arrived. Definitely not! The prophet does not just locate the crisis and foresee the imminent disaster. Nor does he just proclaim the end of the exile. In his message we hear rather that God is the actual active agent of the end; he himself causes it to happen. God does not announce the end out of his ability to foresee it but rather proclaims that he is about to set it in motion. In a word, the content of the prophetic message is not the end itself, but God bringing about that end. Some pertinent passages:

"And I also withheld the rain from you when there were yet three months to the harvest; I would send rain upon one city and send no rain upon another city; one field would be rained upon, and the field on which it did not rain withered; so two or three cities wandered to one city to drink water and were not satisfied; yet you did not return to me," says the Lord. (Am 4:7-8)

"For behold, I will raise up against you a nation, O house of Israel," says the Lord, the God of hosts; "and they shall oppress you from the entrance of Hamath to the brook of the Arabah." (Am 6:14)

Therefore the anger of the Lord was kindled against his people, and he stretched out his hand against them and smote them, and the mountains quaked; and their corpses were as refuse in the midst of the streets. For all this, his anger is not turned away and his hand is stretched out still. (Is 5:25)

He will raise a signal for a nation afar off, and whistle for it from the ends of the earth; and lo, swiftly, speedily it comes! (Is 5:26)

Behold, I am stirring up the Medes against them, who have no regard for silver and do not delight in gold. Their bows will slaughter the young men; they will have no mercy on the fruit of the womb; their eyes will not pity children. And Babylon, the glory of kingdoms, the splendor and pride of the Chaldeans, will be like Sodom and Gomorrah when God overthrew them. (Is 13:17-19)

"Behold, I am bringing upon you a nation from afar, O house of Israel," says the Lord. "It is an enduring nation, it is an ancient nation, a nation whose language you do not know, nor can you understand what they say." (Jer 5:15)

I will come against the wayward people to chastise them... for their double iniquity. (Hos 10:10)

To ensure that Israel and Judah do not misread or misinterpret the facts, the prophets always make it crystal clear that the locusts, the earthquake, the lack of rain, etc., are not simply "natural" phenomena; nor are the movements of the Assyrians, Egyptians, Babylonians, and Medo-Persians merely military, strategic, and political actions—rather, God himself is acting through them. They are effectively his agents carrying out his will.

God Acting Here and Now

This last point brings me to speak of God as the Lord of both creation and history in the prophetic preaching. It is to be noted that the prophets did not deliver lectures. They did not teach that God had created and thus was Creator, or that he had guided

Israel's steps in the past and thus was the Lord of history. Instead they preached God as Creator insofar as he was performing, right then and there, deeds possible only to the Master of all creation. They preached him as God of all nations insofar as he was the master of their individual destinies and was himself making them act in such a manner as to fulfill his intentions.

What made the prophetic word powerful was the fact that it did not present its hearers with an assumed God, a God from the past, but with a God who was proving himself to be just that in the experience of their daily lives. This is not to say the prophets were uninterested in God's past deeds, as if God were appearing for the first time on the historical scene. On the contrary, what the prophet understood was that unless God can prove to be Creator, Redeemer, and Lord today, this very day, then his claim to absolute sovereignty has no basis and the people will be justified in binding him to the rules set down in the past. Such a God was in no way the prophet's Lord!

One Universal God

It is in this line of thought that I understand the place of the oracles against the nations in the prophetic message. The content of each oracle is far less important than the very fact of including the nations surrounding Israel and Judah under the sweeping judgment of God. Judgment is the key word here since a nation does not account for its actions to anyone except its own king or deity. The prophets addressed themselves to the nations on God's behalf and issued judgment against them in his name as an essential part of their message, and this essential part is in fact the universality of God. Its most unambiguous expression is in those prophetic sayings which place Israel and Judah on the same plane as the other nations by attributing to those other nations characteristics usually considered unique to Israel:

"Are you not like the Ethiopians to me, O people of Israel?" says the Lord.

"Did I not bring up Israel from the land of Egypt, and the Philistines from Caphtor, and the Syrians from Kir?" (Am 9:7)

Therefore thus says the Lord of hosts: "Because you have not obeyed my words, behold, I will send for all the tribes of the north," says the Lord, "and for Nebuchadrezzar the king of Babylon, my servant..." (Jer 25:8-9; cf. 27:6)

[I am the Lord] who says of Cyrus: "He is my shepherd, and he shall fulfill all my purpose" (Is 44:28)

Thus says the Lord to his anointed, to Cyrus, whose right hand I have grasped... (Is 45:1)

The first passage equates Israel, the chosen of Yahweh, with one of the farthest away and least known peoples in the Old Testament, the Ethiopians. And it considers the exodus—the very symbol of Israel's uniqueness—comparable to similar experiences of its bitterest enemies, the Philistines and the Syrians. According to Jeremiah, God calls Nebuchadrezzar—the destroyer of Jerusalem and the temple—"my servant"; while according to Isaiah the Lord addresses the gentile king Cyrus as his shepherd and his anointed. To understand the significance of these last two titles, one need only recall that some decades earlier Ezekiel had prophesied that King David himself would be the shepherd whom God would appoint over his sheep to pasture them (34:23). So this prophet whom we customarily call "Second Isaiah"[2] boldly proclaimed the gentile king Cyrus as the hoped-for Messiah of the Lord!

Condemnation of Secularism

As I pointed out earlier, God's "aggressiveness" was evident in the fact that he went out to meet the people in their homes, in the streets, at their workshops, etc., and did not wait for them to come to him at the altars and city gates. By acting in this manner, he meant to put an end to the artificial dichotomy created by man between the religious and the social realms.

2. See Part III.

I hate, I despise your feasts, and I take no delight in your solemn assemblies. Even though you offer me your burnt offerings and your cereal offerings, I will not accept them, and the peace offerings of your fatted beasts I will not look upon. Take away from me the noise of your songs; to the melody of your harps I will not listen. But let justice roll down like waters, and righteousness like an everflowing stream. (Am 5:21-24)

For I desire steadfast love and not sacrifice, the knowledge of God, rather than burnt offerings. (Hos 6:6)

And I said: Hear you heads of Jacob and rulers of the house of Israel! Is it not for you to know justice?—you who hate the good and love the evil, ... who eat the flesh of my people, and flay their skin from off them, and break their bones in pieces, and chop them up like meat in a kettle, like flesh in a caldron. Then they will cry to the Lord, but he will not answer them; he will hide his face from them at that time, because they have made their deeds evil. (Mic 3:1-4)

"What to me is the multitude of your sacrifices?" says the Lord; "I have had enough of burnt offerings of rams and the fat of fed beasts; I do not delight in the blood of bulls, or of lambs, or of he-goats. When you come to appear before me, who requires of you this trampling of my courts? Bring no more vain offerings; incense is an abomination to me. ... Your new moons and your appointed feasts my soul hates; they have become a burden to me, I am weary of bearing them. When you spread forth your hands, I will hide my eyes from you; even though you make many prayers, I will not listen; your hands are full of blood. Wash yourselves; make yourselves clean; remove the evil of your doings from before my eyes; cease to do evil, learn to do good; seek justice, correct oppression; defend the fatherless, plead for the widow." (Is 1:11-16)

To understand God's total rejection of any attitude that would divide and separate the religious and social realms,[3] one should recognize this essentially amounts to idolatry. The notion "holy" or "sacred" primarily means something delineated, specific, set apart, reserved, earmarked—something carved out of the general realm and assigned to the One who is not man so that man may never forget the awe due to God. There are, then, two possible

3. In a very beautiful passage the prophet Hosea seems even to reject any dichotomy between the religious realm and that of nature and creation (4:1-3).

approaches to understanding the nature of a holy place: *either* one may say that the earth is man's and that he assigns some parts of it to meet with the divinity so as to satisfy his needs for a religious sauce over the daily routine of life, *or* one may say that "the earth is the Lord's and the fullness thereof"[4] and that God himself assigns specific meeting places where he can confront man face to face, asking him to give account for his daily life. The first approach is clearly idolatrous because it is man who handles the divinity as he would a fashioned idol.

It appears from the prophetic books that Israel and Judah repeatedly fell into just such an attitude. In that case, any intervention on God's part limited to the assigned grounds, be they altars, city gates, or any other meeting places, would not have corrected anything in the people's mental attitude. The only resort for him was to meet them on the grounds they thought to be theirs only and show them that those areas were also his. He actually moved the encounter between him and them to the real battlefield of faith, the daily routine, where we face God every single second of our life, and we face him in the only "image of God" allowed by God himself: our fellow man. Here we are already at the gates of the New Testament!

Our behavior toward our fellow man seems to be the criterion for God's judgment of us. And since this criterion is universal, God judges not only Israel, but all nations according to it. This is precisely what we find at the opening of the book of the earliest among the prophets, Amos: God judges the nations, one by one, including Israel, on the basis of how they treated their neighbors. This means Yahweh is not only the God of the nations (besides Israel and Judah), but he is in fact their only real God, since he is the *only* One to confront them outside the assigned limits of temples and altars.

This recalls a prior point: the universality of God lies not merely in the fact that he addresses the nations, but in the fact that

4. Ps 24:1. See also Ex 9:29; Deut 10:14.

he addresses them as their judge. Moreover, he is universal because he is a *just* judge, using the same criterion for both Israel and the nations, uniting them beyond any separation by confronting each with God's image found universally in the midst of every nation. Whoever fails to acknowledge this truth is liable to misunderstand the whole of biblical prophetism.

The Call to Repentance

I mentioned earlier that the prophet was a messenger proclaiming the end of a particular situation. Now, an end can only be followed by a new beginning, if it is to be followed by anything at all. But how can a fresh start take place without a drastic change in the conditions that caused the end? If the fresh start took place anyway without such a change, wouldn't the new situation then carry within itself the seeds of its own destruction? This raises the question: What actually had to be changed? What had to be purged or purified for God to enact a new start, one that would not be doomed even before it began? In my last point I pointed out man's evil behavior, but what was the root cause of that behavior? Let us again listen to the prophets themselves:

> Hear, O heavens, and give ear, O earth; for the Lord has spoken: "Sons have I reared and brought up, but they have rebelled against me. The ox knows its owner, and the ass its master's crib; but Israel does not know, my people does not understand." Ah, sinful nation, a people laden with iniquity, offspring of evildoers, sons who deal corruptly! They have forsaken the Lord, they have despised the Holy One of Israel, they are utterly estranged. (Is 1:2-4)

> All this is for the transgression of Jacob and for the sins of the house of Israel. What is the transgression of Jacob? Is it not Samaria? And what is the sin of the house of Judah? Is it not Jerusalem? Therefore I will make Samaria a heap in the open country, a place for planting vineyards; and I will pour down her stones into the valley, and uncover her foundations. All her images shall be beaten to pieces, all her hires shall be burned with fire, and all her idols I will lay waste; for from the hire of a harlot she gathered them, and to the hire of a harlot they shall return. (Mic 1:5-7)

For cross to the coasts of Cyprus and see, or send to Kedar and examine with care; see if there has been such a thing. Has a nation changed its gods, even though they are no gods? But my people have changed their glory for that which does not profit. Be appalled, O heavens, at this, be shocked, be utterly desolate, says the Lord, for my people have committed two evils: they have forsaken me, the fountain of living waters, and hewed out cisterns for themselves, broken cisterns, that can hold no water. (Jer 2:10-13)

For the prophets, the whole misfortune of Israel and Judah was rooted in their apostasy: the people forsook God and their hearts turned away from him. His countenance was no longer the focus of their vision, nor his voice the delight of their ears. He was simply discarded or at best temporarily shelved. Yet the human heart once touched by the Lord's hand becomes incapable of living without a divine touch—so it must look elsewhere if not to Yahweh. That is what Israel and Judah did and that is what the prophets decried as the cause of the coming end:

Your wickedness will chasten you, and your apostasy will reprove you. Know and see that it is evil and bitter for you to forsake the Lord your God; the fear of me is not in you, says the Lord God of hosts. For long ago you broke your yoke and burst your bonds; and you said, "I will not serve." Yea, upon every high hill and under every green tree you bowed down as a harlot. (Jer 2:19-20)

Thus says the Lord: "What wrong did your fathers find in me that they went far from me, and went after worthlessness, and became worthless?" (Jer 2:5)

Indeed, forsaking real love often leads to prostitution; and after having drunk at the source of living waters, every substitute seems but a leaky cistern. Emptiness begets more emptiness and desolation. The only way out of Israel's and Judah's predicament would be a complete turnabout, a total revolution in the heart's orientation:

Return, O Israel, to the Lord your God, for you have stumbled because of your iniquity. Take with you words and return to the Lord; say to him, "Take away all iniquity; accept that which is good and we will render the fruit of our lips. Assyria shall not save us, we will not ride upon horses; and we will say no more 'Our God,' to the work of our hands. In thee the orphan finds mercy." (Hos 14:1-4)

Return, faithless Israel, says the Lord. I will not look on you in anger, for I am merciful, says the Lord; I will not be angry forever. Only acknowledge your guilt, that you rebelled against the Lord your God and scattered your favors among strangers under every green tree, and that you have not obeyed my voice, says the Lord. Return, O faithless children, says the Lord; for I am your Master... (Jer 3:12-14a; see also 3:22-25)

This is not the place to discuss whether the prophets thought the coming destruction would happen only if the people rejected the call for repentance, or if they prophesied God's unconditional judgment which could be followed by a new beginning if conversion were to take place. The point is that repentance, or return to God (*šub, metanoia*), was a sine qua non condition for the new chapter God would consider opening in the story of Israel and Judah, and as such it was an integral part of the prophetic preaching.

Pictures vs. Words

The reader of the prophetic books will quickly notice that symbolism was commonly used as a channel of communication both to the prophets by God and by the prophets to the people around them. Very often God transmitted his word to his messenger through symbolic visions. These are found starting with Amos in the mid-eighth century B.C. all the way down to Zechariah at the end of the sixth century—spanning practically the whole period of classical prophetism. A vision conveys more vividly, more totally, and more immediately the content of a message than words alone would do. The old adage, "a picture is worth a thousand words" comes to mind. And the same principle applies to the message when relayed by the prophets to the people. This explains why all of them used such rich imagery in their preaching, to the extent that their words were much like brushes painting vivid scenes. Some of them (Hosea, Isaiah, Jeremiah, and Ezekiel) even went so far as to physically act out their proclamation. Think of Hosea's wife Gomer; Isaiah walking around naked and barefoot in the city; Jeremiah carrying a yoke around his neck and buying a field in his native town of Anathoth; and the frequent symbolic actions recorded throughout the book of Ezekiel.[5]

The "Pregnant" Word

The intimacy the prophets had with the word of God made them realize how real and effective that word was. Although as men they often felt sadness, bitterness, impatience, and despair in their daily lives as well as in their mission, yet as God's messengers they were familiar with the experience of his word. And one of the things they learned is that because God is not a void, empty, vain idol, he could be relied upon to carry out his promises; his word must be, as it were, "pregnant." The realization of this fact pervades their writings. Although very often they themselves could not see how, when, or where God's word would give birth to its promised action, they were nevertheless firmly convinced through their intimacy with it that it *would* prove itself in due time. It is as if they were more interested in the word itself than in its effects. Because of the depth of their faith in God's word, they continued to hope even when human logic counselled despair.

Two powerful instances should suffice to explicate this point. Jeremiah foretold the siege and ultimate defeat of Jerusalem, yet at the height of that siege he heeded the Lord's call and bought for himself a field in nearby Anathoth as a sign that the people would return (32:1-15). Considering how obvious it was to his contemporaries that all of Judah would soon belong to Babylon and not to the Judahites, his faith in God's word against all the odds of the moment are reflected in what he did.

> I signed the deed, sealed it, got witnesses and weighed the money on scales. Then I took the sealed deed of purchase, containing the terms and conditions, and the open copy; and I gave the deed of purchase to Baruch

5. Hos chs.1 and 3; Is 20:2; Jer 27:2; 28:10; 32:6-15. In Ezekiel see, for example, chs.4-6.

the son of Neriah son of Mahseiah, in the presence of Hanamel my cousin, in the presence of the witnesses who signed the deed of purchase, and in the presence of all the Jews who were sitting in the court of the guard. I charged Baruch in their presence, saying, "Thus says the Lord of hosts, the God of Israel: Take these deeds, both this sealed deed of purchase and this open deed, and put them in an earthenware vessel, that they may last for a long time. For thus says the Lord of hosts, the God of Israel: Houses and fields and vineyards shall again be bought in this land." (vv.10-15)

The second example we find in the attitude of Isaiah at a time when the facts appeared to be going against what the Lord had said:

For the Lord spoke thus to me with his strong hand upon me, and warned me not to walk in the way of this people, saying: "Do not call conspiracy all that this people call conspiracy, and do not fear what they fear, nor be in dread. But the Lord of hosts, him you shall regard as holy; let him be your fear, and let him be your dread. And he will become a sanctuary, and a stone of offense, and a rock of stumbling to both houses of Israel, a trap and a snare to the inhabitants of Jerusalem. And many shall stumble thereon; they shall fall and be broken; they shall be snared and taken." Bind up the testimony, seal the teaching among my disciples. I will wait for the Lord, who is hiding his face from the house of Jacob, and I will hope in him. Behold, I and the children whom the Lord has given me are signs and portents in Israel from the Lord of hosts, who dwells on Mount Zion. (8:11-18)

These two instances show that for God's messenger the Lord's word cannot have any external criterion—it is instead its own criterion. It is true even if everything else seems to prove it false. Faith in God's word gave the prophet *hope* that some day, somehow, it would bear its fruits beyond any human imagination. And so the word was kept in scrolls awaiting the day when it would "become flesh"!

I

The Book of Amos

1

Introductory Material (1:1-2)

Layers of Tradition (1:1a)

Each prophetic book is a compilation of a prophet's speeches or writings, sometimes combined with narratives of his experiences. Each came into being over a period of time as new pieces were added to existing collections or originally separate collections were joined. And here in this verse which serves as the title of the book of Amos we find evidence of that very process. Notice that "The words of Amos, who was among the shepherds of Tekoa" could easily stand alone without the addition of "which he saw concerning Israel in the days of Uzziah king of Judah and in the days of Jeroboam the son of Joash, king of Israel, two years before the earthquake." And notice what that addition does to the verse as a whole. It renders the grammatical construction awkward since there are now two relative clauses referring back to two different nouns ("who was among..." refers to Amos while "which he saw..." refers to his words).[1] Not only does this sound strange, but now we have Amos "seeing" his own "words"![2] It is difficult to imagine someone writing a statement like this from scratch, but these kinds of quirks happen often when an editor adds to an existing text.

So we have in the title clear evidence of at least two stages in the book's formation, and this seems to be confirmed by the text

1. The confusion in relative clauses is even more striking in the original Hebrew. Although in English we immediately know what refers to what because of the difference between "who" and "which," that differentiation has been supplied by the translator. The Hebrew behind those two words is one and the same word 'ašer.

2. To be sure, "seeing a word" does occur elsewhere (Is 2:1; Mic 1:1). However, it is the Lord's word that Isaiah and Micah saw. The awkwardness here lies in the fact that Amos saw his own words.

itself. Chs.3-5 each contain a speech of Amos called a "word,"[3] suggesting that "the words of Amos" in the title may specifically refer to these speeches. If so, the first part of the title and those three speeches may have formed a separate unit at one time. Such an interpretation might stand on shaky ground if it could be shown that "the words of the prophet" is a typical, general formula—but it is not. The books of Hosea and Micah, contemporaries of Amos, prefer a more "theological" formula: "the word [singular] of the Lord [not the prophet] that came to the prophet" (Hos 1:1; Mic 1:1). And that is what appears in nearly all of the other prophetic books.[4] The fact that the editor of Amos did not even combine "the words of the prophet" with "the word of the Lord," as did the editor of Jeremiah,[5] indicates his awareness that "The words of Amos" referred specifically to a collection of "words" in the sense of "speeches."

Of course, the text of Amos as we have it now consists of third-person narrative in addition to first-person speeches. Here too we encounter an interesting quirk. The story of the prophet's "call" is located in chs.7-9, not at the beginning of the book where you would expect to find it. Of the other prophetic books which include a call narrative, all but one are arranged in that more logical manner.[6] Isaiah is the only exception, but even Isaiah is similar to the others insofar as the call in ch.6 (at Uzziah's death) introduces the prophet's activity recorded in chs. 7-12 (under Uzziah's son Ahaz). In the case of Amos, however, the call is relegated to the end of the book; it comes after the activity it should be introducing rather than before it! It is almost as if the account of the call was an afterthought, a late addition to the text of Amos. In contrast, the editor of Isaiah seems to have had the prophet's call in mind from the beginning, despite the presence of

3. See 3:1; 4:1; 5:1.
4. Joel 1:1; Zeph 1:1; Ezek 1:3; Jon 1:1; Hag 1:1; Zech 1:1; Mal 1:1.
5. "The words of Jeremiah...to whom the word of the Lord came..." (1:1-2).
6. Jeremiah, Ezekiel, Hosea, Jonah.

other material preceding the "call" narrative. The title of that book reads: "The vision of Isaiah...which he saw concerning Judah and Jerusalem..." (1:1). The author of that title was apparently a single individual well aware that the call in ch.6 consisted of a "vision," and he chose his terminology accordingly.[7] On the other hand, the editor of Amos—who also naturally wanted to refer to the prophet's call in the title—apparently had to work with an earlier title which he dared not change but which did not mention Amos' call. So he did what he could, the result being the awkward construction whereby "Amos' words" (the original title) were "seen by Amos" himself (a reference to the visions related in the call narrative).

The conclusion pointed to by all these facts is that there was first a collection of Amos' speeches entitled "The words of Amos of Tekoa,"[8] to which a later editor added a collection of narratives about Amos' call and amended the title accordingly. This explains the awkwardness of the title as it stands now. But then why didn't this later editor put the call narratives first, where they belong chronologically? Apparently chronology, and consequently biographical data about Amos as an individual, were both considered less important than Amos' message itself. This emphasis on the prophet's words over his person begins here with Amos and will

---

7. Another indication that the editor formulated his title with the vision of ch.6 in mind can be seen in his inclusion of Uzziah's name in it. According to 6:1 Isaiah began his work after Uzziah's death, so there was no need to include the latter in the list of kings during whose reign Isaiah prophesied. If mention of Uzziah were simply standard procedure for prophets of that time period, we would find it also in the title of the book of Isaiah's contemporary, Micah—but we do not. Therefore "Uzziah" in the title was most likely inspired by "Uzziah" in the "call" narrative.

8. In postulating the original title of this collection I am omitting "who was among the shepherds" which now comes between "Amos" and "of Tekoa" because only in the "call" narrative do we hear of his being a shepherd (7:14). On the other hand I am retaining "of Tekoa" in spite of its present separation from "Amos" because the preposition *min* (from/of) which precedes Tekoa is customarily used between a person's name and home town; see Judg 12:8; 2 Kg 21:19; 23:26. If Tekoa really belonged with "shepherds" one would have expected the preposition *b* (in), as in Jer 1:1: "The words of Jeremiah, the son of Hilkiah, of the priests who were *in* Anathoth ...".

remain a striking feature of all of the prophetic books. Even in those books that open with the prophet's call we find precious little to help us understand the prophet's personality. Jeremiah may seem to be an exception, but even there the reader soon realizes that personal data concerning him are offered only to help explain his prophetic activity. In other words, the interest of those who compiled the material for the prophetic books was primarily—if not exclusively—in the message proclaimed by the prophets rather than in the prophets themselves as noteworthy individuals. This explains why each one's "call" is cast in a way that facilitates understanding his mission rather than his personality.[9]

Beginning and Ending Dates (1:1b)

Amos' editors did, however, see fit to provide some information about him. As in the other books of pre-exilic prophets, the king list serves to specify the time of his activity.[10] In a day when there was no universal dating system, each nation's calendar revolved around its own kings' reigns, as can be seen most plainly in Jeremiah 1:2-3:

> ...the word of the Lord came [to Jeremiah] in the days of Josiah the son of Amon, king of Judah, in the thirteenth year of his reign. It came also in the days of Jehoiakim the son of Josiah, king of Judah, and until the end of the eleventh year of Zedekiah the son of Josiah, king of Judah, until the captivity of Jerusalem in the fifth month.[11]

Since Amos was active only in the kingdom of Israel and since only Jeroboam II, king of Israel, plays a significant role in Amos' prophecy (7:9-11), both the mention of Uzziah, king of Judah, and the precedence given to him over Jeroboam in the title are evidence that the (final) editor of the book was a Judahite.

The title also dates Amos' work by reference to "*the* earth-

9. See comments on ch.7 and on other "call" passages in subsequent prophetic books.
10. Cf. Is 1:1; Hos 1:1; Mic 1:1; Zeph 1:1.
11. The habit of giving more extensive data as found in Jeremiah will be carried on in the exilic and post-exilic periods: see Ezek 1:1ff.; 8:1; 20:1; 24:1; 26:1; 29:1; 31:1; 32:1; 40:1; Hag 1:1; 2:1, 10, 20; Zech 1:1, 7; 7:1.

quake." The definite article with no further specification indicates an event that was well-known and unique. Earthquakes in Palestine are not unusual, but this one must have been in a class all its own, especially since it was still remembered centuries later in the post-exilic book of Zechariah as a model of what would happen on the awesome "day of the Lord," the final day of judgment (14:4-5). One can safely surmise that if Amos himself were still active at the time of such a catastrophe he would certainly have used it in his message of doom against the kingdom of Israel! He must, then, have ceased prophesying some time before the event. That means his prophetic activity could not have lasted more than two years, since he began only "two years before the earthquake." In fact, it could well have covered only a few months: since years were reckoned on a calendar basis, a period spanning parts of two consecutive years could be considered as having taken place over "two years." This actually seems more likely; with the high priest of Bethel ordering him to go home and even accusing him of conspiracy against the king (7:10-13), it hardly seems likely he would have been tolerated in Israel for even one whole year.[12]

The determination that Amos acted as a prophet for such a short period is of interest not just as a matter of idle curiosity; it leads to the important conclusion that one cannot speak of Amos as having *become* a prophet in the sense of accepting a lifetime "calling" or "office." He was a fig-pincher who had something to say, said it, and then was heard from no more. Obviously, this does not accord with the common understanding of "prophet" as a special class of person, and rather than try to force Amos into that mold we must recognize that it doesn't fit.[13]

And there is a more general lesson to be learned here: the length of time expended on a task is not a deciding factor in determining the value of that task from God's perspective. When

12. This conclusion becomes certain if "two years before the earthquake" is taken simply as a reference to the time of Amos' activity, and not to its duration.
13. See also comments on 7:14-15 below.

God sees fit to intervene in human history what matters is the content of his servants' words and actions—be it for a moment or a lifetime.

A Preface (1:2)

Before presenting the words of Amos himself starting in 1:3, the editor advances a summary of the prophet's message phrased as if it were spoken by the prophet himself.[14] Although cast in the classic style of a liturgical hymn, this preface also uses some of Amos' own terminology which is anything but traditional. The traditional aspect of the hymn can be found in the phrase "utters his voice," a common expression in scriptural descriptions of theophanies. Where Amos breaks new ground is in paralleling the Lord's voice with a lion's roar, an idea which appears in 3:8 and is reflected here.[15]

Also quite unconventional was the idea that the Lord's thunderous voice would be destructive rather than beneficent. Until Amos' day, God's anger was always by definition directed against the enemies and oppressors of his people.[16] Thus "the Lord's day" traditionally carried very positive connotations; one would look forward to that day with eager anticipation and would describe it in glowing terms as a bright, happy day. But then Amos turned everything upside down by speaking of it as a day of darkness and gloom (5:18-20; 3:14-15). This is what the editor masterfully

14. The phrase *wayyo'mar* (and he said) is out of place at the beginning of v.2. The conjunction *w* (and) followed by an imperfect verb (normally future tense) having the past perfect sense belongs in a narrative sequence, which is not the case here. The editor obviously intended to link the saying in this verse with the verb *hazah* (he saw) in v.1 to indicate that Amos' message was the outcome of his vision.

15. In this context "voice" means the thunder accompanying divine appearances. See Ps 18:13; 46:6; 104:7; Is 30:30f. "Voice" parallels thunder in Ps 18:13, and Ps 104:7 speaks of the "voice of thy thunder" (RSV substitutes "sound" for "voice" here, but the Hebrew has the same word *qol* which may be translated either way). Jer 25:30 and Joel 3:16 also compare God's voice to a "roar" but are later texts obviously modeled after Am 1:2, and neither expressly identifies the "roar" as that of a "lion."

16. See Ps 18:1-19; 46:1-11; Is 30:29-33.

captured in the second half of his preface by saying, "the pastures of the shepherds mourn, and the top of Carmel withers." Thunder can mean rain which is beneficial to pastures and forests; yet this time it announces drought, destruction, and mourning.

2

Oracles Against the Nations (1:3-2:16)

Here we have a long passage containing Amos' sweeping message of divine judgment against the kingdoms surrounding Israel, leading up to the condemnation of Israel itself. Each nation gets its own oracle, and each oracle (with a few exceptions) follows the same basic pattern: (a) the introductory formula "thus says the Lord"; (b) a statement that God's punishment will not be revoked; (c) the indictment; (d) the sentence called for by the stated offense; (e) the closing formula "says the Lord."

Editorial Additions (1:9-12; 2:4-5)

The oracle against Judah is strikingly different from the others in content. Whereas each other nation is called to account for a specific wrong perpetrated against a third party, the charge against Judah is cast in general terms reminiscent of the vocabulary and style of Deuteronomy: Judah's transgression is not in oppressing its neighbors but in rejecting the law of the Lord, neglecting his statutes, and following after "lies," i.e., idols (2:4).[1] God's sentence of judgment upon Judah is also different in that the statement about sending fire to devour the strongholds of the capital (2:5) is not elaborated upon as it is elsewhere (1:4-5; 1:7-8; 1:14-15; 2:2-3); it seems terse and unimaginative by comparison. In 1:4 the fire is sent upon the house of King Hazael (not Syria) to destroy the strongholds of King Ben-Hadad (not Damascus). In 1:7 the fire is sent upon the "wall" of the capital. In 1:14 it is

1. Compare with Deut 4:1, 5, 14, 40; 5:1, 7, 31; 6:1, 14, 17, 24; 7:3-4, 11, 16, 25; 8:19; 11:32; 12:1; 16:12; 17:18-19; 26:16, 17; 27:10; 27:26; 28:58; 29:29; 30:10; 31:12; 32:46.

"kindled" rather than "sent." In 2:2, it is not Moab's capital Kir-hare-seth[2] whose strongholds are to be devoured, but rather Kerioth, the central shrine of Moab's god Chemosh. In contrast, Judah's sentence strictly follows the basic formula: fire upon the nation to devour the strongholds of the capital. So the oracle against Judah stands out from the others—but why? Amos himself was never interested in Judah; his preaching was directed exclusively at the northern kingdom of Israel, never at its sister to the south.[3] The explanation that best fits the facts: this oracle did not actually originate with Amos but is the product of an editor who intended to adapt Amos' words against Israel to the situation obtaining in Judah a century later, during or after Josiah's Deuteronomic reform.[4] In effect, this editor did what every preacher does today with Scripture: reinterpreted it in order to make it speak to his contemporaries.

The oracles against Tyre (1:9-10) and Edom (1:11-12) appear more like the one against Judah than the others in that they too omit the closing "says the Lord" and keep the punishment sentence to a terse minimum (compare 1:10 and 12 with 2:5). Their indictments read more like Judah's, too. For Damascus, Philistia, Ammon, and Moab, the named offense consists of two phrases portraying one transgression.[5] But the charge against Edom, like Judah's, is composed of four parts. And the charge against Tyre, although it does contain only two parts, is different from the others in that its second segment is not merely the second half of one descriptive sentence but instead reinterprets the first half which is complete in itself.[6] Consequently, one is led to suspect

2. See Is 16:7, 11; Jer 48:31, 36.
3. See 1:1; 3-5; 6:6, 8, 14; 7:1-9:8. I shall deal with the apparent exception 6:1 in its own time.
4. See vol.1, pp.71-77.
5. See the text immediately following "because" in 1:3d; 6d; 13d; 2:1d.
6. Besides, the first segment is an almost verbatim repetition of the indictment against Gaza (1:6d). Literally, 1:6d reads: "Because they exiled into exile an entire population to deliver them to Edom," while 1:9d reads: "Because they delivered into exile an entire population to Edom." The latter version is smoother than the former and therefore probably later; literary improvement is usually the result of editorial activity.

that the oracles against Tyre and Edom are later additions from the time of the Deuteronomistic editor who added the oracle against Judah (or shortly thereafter).

This conclusion is supported by the historical data of the period. Edom's "brother" in 1:11 must be none other than either Israel or Judah since Edom is another name for Esau, the brother of Jacob/Israel[7] and by extension of the latter's son, Judah. Apparently, then, a Judahite is charging Edom with a heinous offense against Judah, resentfully depicting Edom as some kind of rapacious, heartless monster. There is just one period of history when such feelings of a Judahite against Edom would be understandable, and it comes only after the Babylonian exile. During David's time Edom had been totally subjugated to Judah (2 Sam 8:13-14) and did not recover until the fall of Jerusalem in 587 B.C. It was then that Edom saw its opportunity to break the Judean yoke and even invade its former conqueror. Hence a psalm otherwise directed against Babylon also castigates Edom (137:7), and a book lamenting the fall of Jerusalem also promises retribution for Edom (Lam 4:21-22). Hence also the lengthy oracles against Edom by prophets who witnessed that catastrophe (Jer 49:7-22; Ezek 25:12-14; 35:1-15). The entire book of Obadiah decries Edom's aggression.[8] The city-state of Tyre became prominent in the same time period, around the beginning of the 6th century B.C., and the fact that it engaged in similarly disreputable behavior can easily be gathered from Ezekiel's five oracles against it (26:1-14; 26:15-21; 27:1-36; 28:1-10; 28:11-19).

---

7. See Gen 25:30; 36:1, 8, 19.

8. The experience of Edom's "betrayal" of Judah lingered for centuries in the memory of Judahites, as is evident from the late post-exilic prophecy of Malachi (Mal 1:2-5).

The Oracles Against Neighboring Nations (1:3-8; 1:13-2:3)

From the foregoing we can conclude that Amos' authentic oracles are those against Damascus, Philistia, Ammon, Moab, and Israel. Each of them uses the first person singular on behalf of God and brackets his words between the expressions "Thus says the Lord" and "says the Lord." The bracketing expressions are part of a standard format termed the "messenger speech" and function as our quotation marks do: they separate a verbatim quotation of the sender from any further personal comments the messenger might make. Amos' use of the "messenger speech" here indicates that in the delivery of these oracles he saw himself as God's extraordinary emissary. And he saw his message not as the questionable opinion of a human being but as the undebatable and unappealable judgment of the One who exercises absolute and final authority over all human beings—God himself.

The literary device of numerical gradation ("n and n+1") is a well-known feature of wisdom literature.[9] It is used either to express the completeness of a series of related elements or to emphasize the last in such a series.[10] When the series refers to similar elements, only the last of which is named, the intention is to say that the measure of something has reached its ultimate degree. That is what we have in Amos' oracles, where in each case it is the fourth and last transgression that was the "straw that broke the camel's back" and called down God's wrath upon the transgressor.

In each instance the effect of that wrath is not a slap on the wrist but actually the annihilation of the transgressor. An overreaction on God's part? Not if we understand the meaning of *pešaʿ*,

9. Most common are the sequences two-three (Sir 23:16-21; 26:28; 50:25; see also Eccl 4:12), three-four (Pr 30:15, 18, 21, 29; Sir 26:5-6), and six-seven (Pr 6:16).
10. For examples of the former usage see Prov 6:16-19; 30:15-16, 18-19, 21-23, 29-31. A good example of the latter is Sir 23:16-21 where, after the short criticisms of onanism (v.16b) and fornication (v.17), the condemnation of adultery spans four verses (vv.18-21); see also Sir 26:5-6, 28.

the Hebrew word translated "transgression." This word, like the "n and n+1" literary device, stems from traditional wisdom, whose origin is in tribal society. In that context the reference is to actions that threaten the volatile harmony necessary for the permanence of tribal—and later civilized—life.[11] Such actions amount to a revolt against the person functioning as the guarantor of this harmony, i.e., the patriarch in a clan or tribe (and later the king in a city-state). Any such revolt is literally catastrophic since it threatens not only the welfare but also the very being of the tribe or clan. In tribal society, the patriarch personifies the source of communitarian order that secures the ongoing existence of his tribe. In order to maintain an orderly social life, there can be no more than one source of authority, and any revolt against that source is equivalent to a blow at the very root of society. Revolt against a tribal patriarch can thus be compared to an attempt to overthrow the constitution of a modern democracy. It is understandable then that the only solution to any *pešaʿ* is the elimination of its perpetrator, the alternative being the disintegration of tribal society itself. And when an entire society commits a *pešaʿ*— let alone four—then it has committed suicide. Divine intervention merely carries out the self-destructive will of the transgressor!

The four nations addressed by Amos are the immediate neighbors and traditional foes of Israel: Syria, Philistia, Ammon, and Moab. The specific aggressive actions being condemned must have taken place during a window of opportunity created by a weakened Assyrian empire in the first half of the eighth century B.C. The scope of this book does not allow a detailed discussion of each of these instances; what is relevant, though, is that in each case Amos speaks of a wrong done not to Israel but to another nation. This is not a case of God avenging wrongs perpetrated against "his own people." Even in the unlikely event that the

11. See the strictures against strife of all kinds in Prov 10:11-12, 19-21; 12:13; 17:9, 19; 19:11; *28:2*, 13, *24*; 29:6-7, 16, 22.

"whole people" in 1:6b means Israel or Judah,[12] and if Gilead in 1:3b and 13b is meant as part of Israel rather than as a separate entity,[13] there still remains the unequivocal statement in 2:1 indicting Moab for a transgression against *Edom*—Israel's and Judah's perennial enemy. Why would Israel's national god concern himself with other nations' affairs which have no effect on Israel whatsoever? The only answer is that from Amos' perspective, Israel's "national god" considers himself also to be the god of each of the four surrounding nations as well. The basic function of a nation's deity is to act as its just judge,[14] and in these oracles the Lord acts as the "just judge" of the surrounding nations no less than of Israel.

Let us imagine then the scenario that took place when Amos spoke these words in Israel.[15] His listeners would have been thrilled to hear this stranger[16] proclaim that Yahweh himself was going to smite their enemy Damascus (1:3-5) for a sin it committed against Gilead. They would certainly have welcomed anyone, even a stranger, to proffer such paeans of praise for their own god's invincible power, especially in an announcement of destruction for one of their hated foes. They were all ears for more, and Amos delivered: two similar proclamations of God's intervention were forthcoming, one against the Philistine cities (1:6-8) and one against Ammon (1:13-15). One can imagine the growing crowd of Israelites listening with approval to this person who was indeed obviously speaking the words of God. Perhaps they even hoped Moab's turn would be next, and so it was. But here was a fly in the ointment—Moab's transgression was against

12. Which is hard to imagine since both Israel and Judah were at the zenith of their power in the first half of the 8th century. And a reference to pre-Davidic times (when the Philistines were harassing Dan, Judah, Benjamin, and Ephraim) is not likely because all of Amos' other oracles address contemporary events.

13. Which is possible but cannot be proved beyond a doubt.

14. See Ps 9:4, 7-8; 11:4-5; 45:6-7a; 89:14a; 97:2a; see also Ps 122:5.

15. Either at Bethel (see Am 7:13), or at Samaria if one assumes he must have preached in the capital city some of the oracles leveled against it or the nation as a whole (e.g., Am 3:9-11; 4:1-3; 5:2-3; 6:1-7).

16. Keep in mind Amos was a Judahite (Am 1:1; 7:12) who travelled north to say his piece.

Israel's perennial enemy, Edom. Surely Amos could have thought of many better reasons to condemn Moab, but if this "man of God" put it that way, so be it. Everything else he said sounded good. "And after all," the Israelites might have thought, "this just shows how the Lord our God judges with equity even when it comes to the other nations' squabbles among themselves; he judges everyone by the same criterion of how they treat their neighbors, and it just goes to show that our God is over all."

The Oracle Against Israel (2:6, 13-16)

Suddenly Amos struck his audience with the unexpected: this just judge of a God was planning to strike down *Israel too* after having applied to it the same criterion used against the other nations! And this last condemnation in fact differed not one whit from the others—the same "messenger formula" bracketing God's own words (2:6a, 16c), the same irrevocability of punishment (2:6bc), the same sentence of annihilation (2:13-16), and all because of the same mistreatment of one's "neighbor" (2:6de-8). However, a closer look at the indictment of Israel in 2:6-8 will reveal the following distinguishing characteristic. Israel's transgression is, as it were, internalized: it is not between Israel and a foreign nation but takes place entirely within Israel. The other nations could plead extenuating circumstances because what God considered "neighbors" were, after all, foreign peoples, i.e., potential or even actual enemies. Israel, on the other hand, had not even such a flimsy excuse: the one God calls "neighbor" is simply a fellow Israelite, a neighbor in the simplest, most literal sense. And consequently the misconduct within Israel amounts to a *pešaʿ* in the truest sense of the word. Since the Israelites are "brothers" of the one family (clan/tribe) whose patriarch is God, any lack of brotherly care threatens the family order and jeopardizes its very existence, *including* the person of its patriarch. That this perception of Israel according to clan terminology was in fact in Amos' purview can be gathered from his first "word" where Israel is addressed as one of the *mišpahot* (families, clans) of the earth (3:2).

It appears then that only Israel's transgression is truly a *peša'* in the strict sense of the word; and if this is true, then the oracles against the surrounding nations were devised only as a preamble to the one against Israel. Several other factors support that conclusion:

1) No attempt was made to convince the other nations themselves of anything—the oracles against them were spoken exclusively to the nation of Israel. Therefore the only purpose those oracles serve is to help convince Israel that the Lord means business, that he considers Israel's transgression no less serious than that of these other nations.

2) As in Israel's case, the punishments against the nations are stated using the Hebrew imperfect mood which normally corresponds to the English future tense.[17] In other words, they are threats and not references to punishments already effected. There is not even a suggested sequence of events, no indication that Israel could expect to receive its punishment only after the others. So Amos is not saying, "look what has happened or will happen to them to see what will happen to you," but rather, "God will judge you, Israel, as harshly as he will judge the nations." He mentions the nations only to show that Israel will be treated no differently from them.

3) Starting with ch.3 Amos' concern is exclusively with Israel. Not only in content but also in length, the oracles against the nations constitute only a preamble to the main message.

As for the content of the oracle against Israel, let us begin with the authentic words of Amos preserved in 2:6 and 13-16 (as I will show below, the intervening material is composed of later editorial additions intended to enhance Amos' message and make it relevant to subsequent Judahite audiences). The original indictment against Israel is in v.6b, and it concerns the malfeasance of those in charge of justice. There is more to this than the obvious

17. See "I will not revoke it [the punishment]" and "I will send/kindle a fire..." throughout this section, as well as the future tense in 1:5, 7, 15; 2:3, 5, 13-16.

evil of injustice, however. Recall that the dispensing of just judgments was the main function of any national god in the ancient Near East, since the deity was naturally patterned after the image of a king. This means the office of judge—assumed mainly by the king but also by the elders and priests—was a "divine" office in the sense that the judge was the earthly representative carrying out the deity's responsibilities. The judge's verdicts, then, necessarily reflected directly on the deity in behalf of which he acted. And unjust verdicts tarnished any image people might have had of the deity itself as a "just judge." Consequently, "selling the righteous for silver" in Israel makes a mockery of Yahweh; it means either he has no power to control his representatives or he is actually not so just after all. This cannot help but undermine his authority within his domain—and that is the very definition of *pešaʿ* as pointed out earlier. This is an extremely serious offense whose remedy cannot be anything less than the radical elimination of the whole judicial apparatus in Israel—king, palace administrators, elders, and priests. In practical terms, this amounts to the elimination of the entire kingdom, Yahweh's kingdom. An action of such magnitude would have to be warranted and well justified. How did Amos— or Yahweh on whose behalf he was speaking—go about ensuring that his accusation was irrefutable?

The key to understanding this poetic section of Amos lies in recognizing the "synonymic parallelism" it shares with the rest of Hebrew poetry. Synonymic parallelism is a literary device whereby each verse consists of two lines which are parallel in that they express the same thought using different words. Psalm 51 provides an obvious and well-known example:

> Have mercy on me, O God, according to thy steadfast love;
>> according to thy abundant mercy blot out my transgressions.

> Wash me thoroughly from my iniquity,
>> and cleanse me from my sin!

> For I know my transgressions,
>> and my sin is ever before me.

Against thee, thee only, have I sinned,
   and done that which is evil in thy sight,
   so that thou art justified in thy sentence
   and blameless in thy judgment.

Behold, I was brought forth in iniquity,
   and in sin did my mother conceive me. (vv.1-5)

Amos' indictment against Israel shows the same structure:

because they sell the righteous for silver
   and the needy (*'ebyon*) for a pair of shoes (2:6b)

Here "needy" in the second line is the counterpart of "righteous" in the first. This does not mean that Amos is speaking about the needy righteous or the righteous needy, but rather that righteous and needy are equivalent. In Amos' eyes—*and thus in Yahweh's!*—the righteous *is* the needy, or, more precisely, the needy, and only he, *is* the righteous. How is one to account for this one-sidedness? Is justice bound by poverty? What about the rich? Are they ipso facto unrighteous?

Although such questions seem self-evident and compelling to our modern mind, they are in reality irrelevant to the point that Amos— on behalf of God—is trying to make. His goal is not to decide who is righteous or unrighteous but to present irrefutable proof that there is *pesa'* in Israel. To do that he needs to demonstrate convincingly that there is injustice in it. And if his audience knows that poor people get short shrift in Israelite courts, he only needs to refer to that fact. The acquittal of a rich person *may* be due to bribery, but this cannot be the case for a poor person—so the acquittal of a poor person would testify to the untainted justice of the court.[18] Consequently, only when a poor person is innocent and proclaimed so by the court is there objective proof that the court judges rightly and so is in fact administering "divine" justice. Conversely, if poor people are never exonerated the presumption must be that this is due to injustice and therefore *pesa'*.

Israel's punishment described in vv.13-16 originally followed v.6. V.13 announces the destruction the Lord himself will bring

18. As with all generalizations, there are of course exceptions, such as when the accused is a relative of the judge; nevertheless, the generalization as such is true.

down upon Israel, and vv.14-16 portray the result of that action in terms of an army in total disarray: even the elite troops will be put to shame by being stripped entirely of their armor. What a punishment and what a sight! The Lord, "the God of hosts,"[19] the supreme commander of the troops of Israel, will attack and destroy his own army![20]

An Editor's Comments (2:7-12)

The editorial additions in vv.7-12 underscore the magnitude of Israel's *peša'*. V.7a is composed of authentic words of Amos from elsewhere (see 4:1b; 5:11a, 12b; 8:4). It extends the synonymic parallelism of *saddiq* (righteous) and *'ebyon* (needy) to two other words that occur frequently in Amos' message: *dal* (poor/humble) and *'anaw* (afflicted/oppressed). They convey the same message that the courts of Israel are rotten and do not reflect the Lord's just judgment and fatherly care for his people.

Vv.7b-8 refer to three actions strictly prohibited by the law which nevertheless go unchallenged in Israel. Their intent is to show that Israel's sin is an open challenge to God's most divine characteristic of holiness.[21] The first (v.7b) is explicitly called a profanation of his holy name, while the second (v.8a) and third (v.8b) are connected with the altar and the temple, the locales where God's holiness is revealed.

The following two verses (9-10) are the work of editors of the Deuteronomistic school. They highlight Israel's sin by contrasting it with the exodus and the gift of the "promised land." According to Deuteronomy these are the events that bond Israel with its god Yahweh: at the exodus he brought Israel into being, and through his gift of the land he makes it possible for Israel to continue to live as a nation. But now by committing *peša'* Israel is condemning itself to

19. See Am 3:13; 5:14, 15, 16, 27; 6:8, 14. The Hebrew *saba'* can also be translated "army" (i.e., "host of fighting men").
20. See also comments on 5:17 and 18.
21. See 4:2 where the Lord swears by his holiness, i.e., his most inner being.

exile from the land and thus annihilation from existence—the very reverse of what happened at the exodus. This is nothing less than undoing God's work. And compounding Israel's culpability in this evil act is the fact that it had been forewarned by God's special appointees, the Nazirites and the prophets (v.11). Israel ignored them all (v.12).

3

The Three "Words" (3:1-5:6; 5:8-9)

As I explained in my comments on 1:1, the original compendium of Amos' oracles against Israel began with sayings that were gathered in three "words," or sets of speeches. Each of the "words" seems to have been composed of one saying against the nation's capital, Samaria, and another against its official religious center, Bethel.[1] This division is obvious in ch.4 and ch.5,[2] but ch.3 is more complex. Due to its present position as the first or introductory "word," it was given the additional task of presenting in a nutshell Amos' entire message.[3] Besides an oracle against Samaria (3:9-11) and another against Bethel as well as an oracle against Israel in general (vv.13-15), it contains an opening statement (vv.1-2), a series of proverbs (vv.3-8), and an independent short saying (v.12).

Announcement of Punishment (3:1-2)

The abrupt shift from Amos as speaker in v.1a to the Lord as speaker in v.1b is evidence that the latter is an editorial expansion. If v.1b were original one would have expected a "he" in place of the "I," so the original text of this opening statement must be contained in vv.1a and 2. It informs the people of the northern

1. Unlike the southern kingdom of Judah where the capital Jerusalem was also the site of the central temple, in the northern kingdom of Israel there were two centers, one political and one religious. This development is historically explainable since Bethel had all along been a traditional religious center even since patriarchal times, whereas Samaria was chosen as the royal city much later; it followed Tirzah as capital of Israel (1 Kg 15:33; 16:24, 29).

2. 4:1-3 and 5:1-2 are against Samaria/Israel, while 4:4-5 and 5:4-5 are against Bethel.

3. Similar summaries can be found in Hos 1-3; Is 1; Jer 1.

kingdom of Israel that their punishment will take into account "all" their iniquities since they were recognized in a special way by Yahweh out of "all" the families of the earth. The message here corresponds to what was said in the previous oracle against Israel (2:6, 13-16): because Yahweh is Israel's deity, its *pešaʿ* is a direct challenge to his authority and consequently he has no choice but to eradicate the *pešaʿ* under *all* its aspects, i.e., to punish Israel for *all* its sins.

Much of the powerful impact of the original poetry is lost in translation. The Hebrew verb *paqad*, usually translated "punish," actually means "visit." It is commonly used to speak of a deity's beneficent visitation to its people gathered at the deity's shrine or temple. Amos' hearers were lulled into a false sense of security by a statement that initially sounded positive—as if it was going to promise them good things—right up until the last word, "iniquities," was uttered. Had the message begun with an unambiguously negative word they might have decided to turn away and shut their ears to avoid hearing it, but Amos phrased it so that by the time they realized what they were hearing it was already too late: the message had been delivered and they had heard it.

The function of the editorial expansion in v.1b was to update Amos' message by making it apply to "the whole family" brought out of Egypt, thereby including the southern kingdom of Judah as a target of Yahweh's threat. This was necessary after the fall of Israel in 722/21 B.C. because Judahites considered their neighbor to the north a renegade that had received its just desserts for the sin of seceding from the Davidic realm after Solomon's death.[4] A condemnatory message aimed solely at their vanquished enemy would only have confirmed them in their own self-righteous attitudes. In other words, Amos' "woe" would have functioned in complete opposition to its original purpose. Paradoxically then, an editorial *change* was necessary in order to preserve the *original* intention! With the addition of v.1b Amos' words stung the ears

4. See 1 Kg 12.

of Judahites at the end of the 7th century B.C. in the same way they did those of Israelites 150 years earlier. And although the message itself was unchanged, its effect on its hearers no doubt was more powerful the second time around. After all, the original Israelite hearers of Amos could take a chance and ignore his threats without worrying too much about something for which there was absolutely no precedent—how could Yahweh strike down his own people Israel? But for the later Judahites things were not so simple, because for them the unthinkable had already happened; a precedent had been established for the unprecedented. Yahweh did destroy Israel, and who could say with confidence he wouldn't do the same to Judah? And after the fall of Jerusalem, the exilic and post-exilic Judahites will have found Amos' oracle of doom still more frightening, since they themselves had experienced the beginning of the threatened punishment and could only look forward to more.

Warnings Against Heedlessness (3:3-8)

Well aware that the natural response to bad news is to "shoot the messenger" and ignore the message, in this passage Amos points out the folly of that response. The rhetorical questions in vv.3-5 prepare the way for his main point by offering a simple reminder of the general principle that everything has a cause. Having attained his audience's assent to the common-sense proposition that things don't "just happen" for no reason, in v.6 Amos applies the principle directly to them: war has been declared against Samaria and it is the Lord himself who has declared it.[5] What then is Amos' role in this declaration of war? V.8 focuses on the fact that the decision rests with God alone, and in proclaiming it Amos is only his messenger, a servant who himself has no choice but to proclaim the will of his master.[6]

---

5. The trumpet has throughout history warned citizens of imminent danger, such as the attack of an enemy, and in the ancient Near East whenever a city was destroyed in a battle it was assumed that its deity must have either allowed or willed it.

6. See more on this notion of Amos' feeling *compelled* to proclaim the divine message in my discussion of his "call" in 7:1-8:3; 9:1-4.

We have in v.7 an editor's attempt to explain that Amos spoke of himself and was justified in doing so when he said, "The Lord God has spoken; who can but prophesy?" (v.8b) Several aspects of its form and content reveal it to be an editorial addition:

1) Formally, it disrupts the flow of rhetorical questions and answers; omit it and the passage reads smoothly from beginning to end. This is an extended parenthetical explanation[7] in contrast to the steady repetition of brief questions and answers in the rest of the passage.

2) The Amos who so emphatically refuses to be called a prophet in 7:14 is not likely to have obliquely called himself one here. Likewise, the Amos who preached the absolute freedom of the Lord to do as he willed is hardly likely to have bound him to the requirement of not doing anything without informing his servants. V.7 presents a picture of an unchanging, predictable deity, while the "national god" who surprises everyone by deciding to destroy his own nation is anything but predictable.

3) The technical appellation "the prophets," especially "God's servants the prophets," came into common usage centuries after Amos' time.[8]

The scenario evoked by the word *sod* (counsel)[9] is that of God's heavenly council debating an issue, reaching a decision, and revealing its decision to special human messengers whose task it will be to proclaim it to other human beings.[10]

---

7. Indicated by the initial word *ki* which may mean "surely" (RSV) or "for" but in either case introduces what follows as a comment on, or explanation of, what precedes. Note also that v.7 begins with the verb '*asah* (to do), again suggesting that it is intended to comment upon v.6 which ends with the same verb.

8. It does not appear until Jeremiah (7:25; 25:4; 26:5; 29:19; 35:15; 44:4) and Ezekiel (38:17), and shows up again centuries later in Daniel (9:6, 10).

9. Rendered "secret" or "plan" in some translations.

10. See 1 Kg 22:19-23, where the entire scenario is described in detail.

Excursus: The Heavenly Council

The members of the divine council were originally considered to be deities themselves; see Job 1:6; Ps 29:1; 82:1; 89:6. They were gradually scaled down to the status of angels or "heavenly hosts," i.e., servants of the one God and thus essentially inferior to him. This happened under the influence of the monotheistic tendency of nascent Judaism in the post-exilic period.[11] Direct evidence of the change can be found in Ps 8:5, which reads "little less than the gods"[12] in the original Hebrew but "little less than the angels" in the much later Septuagint (LXX) translation. See also Deut 32:8 where "according to the number of the sons of gods" is the original reading preserved in the Dead Sea scrolls and the LXX, while the later version found in the Masoretic Hebrew text is "according to the number of the sons of Israel." This later version does not even make sense in the context.

The Lord's Lawsuit (3:9-11)

This first oracle is presented in the form of a lawsuit brought against Samaria by Amos acting on the Lord's behalf. Before proclaiming the indictment (v.10) and its penalty (v.11), he calls for witnesses (v.9a), as required by common ancient Near Eastern legal practice.[13] And an ironic choice of witnesses it is; these are not neutral observers but Israel's bitterest enemies, two powers who had threatened its very birth as a nation at the time of the exodus and who remained antagonistic ever after—Philistia, represented by Ashdod,[14] and

11. See vol.1, pp.121-26.
12. Or "little less than God" as in RSV.
13. See Deut 17:6; 19:15.
14. I follow the LXX text which reads "Ashdod" over against the Hebrew which has "Assyria." The former is clearly the *lectio difficilior*. If "Assyria" were the original it would be hard to imagine a later copyist emending it to "Ashdod": after Amos' day Assyria became one of the traditional enemies of Israel and Judah, whereas Philistia hardly represented a threat at all. For the same reason, on the other hand, a Judahite copyist would understandably have "corrected" *'ašdod* into *'aššur* (Assyria) since the Hebrew letter *d* can easily be mistaken for both *u* and *r*.

Egypt. It is as if the shepherd were inviting the wolves to witness the butchering of the sheep and perhaps even join the feast!

Israel's crime is "oppression." The rich and powerful are building up their wealth in the strongholds[15] of the city at the expense of the poor and helpless.[16] The punishment fits the crime: they will see those strongholds torn down and plundered and will find themselves utterly bereft of all their ill-gotten gains.

Interestingly, Amos does not name the adversary who will besiege and plunder the city. Whether he was thinking of Assyria as early as 750 B.C. or not, we shall never know. What is striking, however, is that he does not say so explicitly either here or anywhere else in this book. His silence on such an important point suggests a deliberate attempt to emphasize the fact that Israel's coming misfortune is the work of the Lord himself, regardless of who carries out that work. The earthly power which will attack Israel will only be an agent of his will.[17] This would explain why even later editors who obviously knew of Assyria's invasion of Israel did not insert that name into the text—they understood Amos' intent and deliberately refrained from clarifying a detail at the expense of the main point's clarity.

Emphasis on the Completeness of Destruction (3:12)

Here is an originally independent oracle inserted by an editor between one against Samaria (vv.9-11) and one against Bethel and Israel (vv.13-15). It is commonly misunderstood as offering a ray of hope amid the condemnations, as introducing the notion of

15. The Hebrew word *'armᵉnot* (strongholds) refers to the towers along the fortified walls of a city. Due to their curved shape they strengthen an otherwise much weaker straight wall as well as allow the defenders to have a better view of, and aim at, the assailants. Unfit to function as living quarters, these towers were usually used to store food and ammunition. Hence their connection with the notions of power and richness.

16. See also 2:6-7 and 4:1.

17. See comments on 2:13-16.

"the remnant" which God will save from the calamity to become the basis for a rebirth of his people. But consider the metaphor carefully and a different message becomes clear. Do two legs or a piece of an ear amount to a viable remainder of a sheep? Hardly. The only positive note here is that such "remnants" prove the shepherd's conscientiousness and honesty—they can serve as tangible evidence that he did not simply forsake the sheep to the lion but rather did his best to defend it, and that he didn't just steal the missing animal. As for the sheep itself, the remains are merely evidence of its *total* destruction. The same applies to the corner of a couch and part of a bed: these are not "remnants" in the optimistic theological sense of modern interpretation, but "remains" in the more realistic sense of minimal evidence that what is now a pile of rubble was once a house that has now been *totally* destroyed. Such remains are necessary from Amos' point of view because without them one might never know that destruction took place. Israel's punishment is meant to be more obvious than that.

God Will Abandon His Sanctuary (3:13-15)

An oracle against Bethel (v.14bc) is embedded in one against the northern kingdom in general, termed the house of Jacob[18] as well as Israel. V.14a refers to the day when the Lord will come to visit his people, a day Israel looks forward to as a day of vindication and reward for well-doing but which Amos says will be a day of punishment.[19] Israel's punishment is to begin with the destruction of the horns of the altar of Bethel (v.14cd).[20] The horns of an

18. See Ps 78 and vol.1, pp.27-31.

19. The day of punishment is identified as "the day of the Lord" in 5:18ff.; regarding Israel's positive expectations for it, see comments on 3:1-2.

20. Since in v.14c there is mention of one altar, and since for the single sanctuary of Bethel we would only expect there to be one altar, the plural "altars" in v.14b must be editorial. Following the Deuteronomistic tendency to disparage the northern kingdom and Bethel as its main sanctuary, speaking of many altars at Bethel is tantamount to accusing it of polytheism. The same intent seems to be present in the mention of "every" altar in v.8a that is part of the editorial addition of vv.7b-8.

altar are its most sacred spot and reflect its effectiveness as the deity's point of contact with its people.[21] Since an ineffective altar is no altar at all and since the altar is the point of divine visitation, what Amos is saying amounts to declaring the de facto absence of God from the midst of his people in the northern kingdom of Israel. In a striking reversal of expectations, God's appearance at his main sanctuary will be for the purpose of causing his permanent disappearance from it!

The second result of the Lord's visitation is a corollary of the first: if God will be absent then his kingdom will collapse, starting with the capital Samaria. In that capital, the targets of God's wrath are more particularly the large houses of ivory, symbols of excessive affluence and the violence and robbery used to attain it (v.10; see also 5:11).

As in 2:6, once again it is the poor who are the objectively righteous ones in the Lord's suit against his people. And as was the case in 2:13-16, here again it is God himself, without any intermediary, who will smite both Bethel and Samaria.

The Cows of Bashan (4:1-3)

Chapter four contains the second "word" of Amos, comprised of one oracle against Samaria (vv.1-3), one against Bethel (vv.4-5), and editorial additions in vv.6-13.

The first oracle addresses the wives of the rich in Samaria with the derogatory epithet "cows of Bashan." Bashan is a region located in what is now southwestern Syria, which was a very fertile plain famous for its wheat, oaks, and cattle. The cedars of Lebanon and the oaks of Bashan were both symbols of sturdiness, power, and perfection for the ancient Hebrews—and consequently also of loftiness, pride, and arrogance.[22] By the same

21. Imagine an altar as a large cube of stone, then on the otherwise flat top of it raise each of the four corners slightly. These are the "horns." On their key role in sacrificial rites see Ex 30:10; Lev 4:7, 18, 25, 30, 34: 8:15; 9:9; 16:18. See also 1 Kg 1:50-51; 2:28.

22. See Ezek 27:5-6; Is 2:12-13.

token the bulls of Bashan were symbols of strong and fierce enemies.[23] Thus, the expression "cows of Bashan" not only refers to the power that the wives of the rich could wield but also decries their behavior as inimical. And once again the objects of oppression—the victims of the cows of Bashan—are none other than the poor and the needy. The parallelism in v.1 between the actions of oppressing (*'ašaq*) and crushing (*rasas*) on the one hand, and of feasting on the other, is a clear indication that in Amos' mind affluence and oppression of the poor are interrelated.

The message Amos is sending to the rich women of Samaria is that God has taken a solemn oath that their city would be besieged, attacked, its walls breached, and they themselves would be taken captive and exiled. This promise is irreversible since the Lord swore to it by his own holiness, i.e., by his divine self. Here again, as in 3:11, Amos identifies neither the invader nor the land of exile, although he does specify the direction of their exile as toward "Harmon." Harmon is a mountain in present-day southern Lebanon which in Amos' day delineated the northernmost border of the kingdom of Israel, so the expression *haharmonah* (toward/in the direction of Harmon) is a general one meaning simply "beyond Israel's border toward the north."

God Rejects the Israelites' Sacrifices (4:4-5)

This oracle against Bethel is strikingly potent. In it Amos parodies the priestly call to the people to come forward and offer their sacrifices to the Lord. His parody intentionally transforms that call into a sarcastic description of what their sacrifices really are in the eyes of God: *peša'* against God! What makes this message even more dreadful is that it is presented as a messenger speech, i.e., as if God himself were speaking directly through Amos. In other words, God himself is rejecting their sacrifices as worse than worthless, as themselves *peša'*. And it is not as though they don't

23. See Ps 22:12-13.

really realize what they are doing, the fact is they *love* to transgress in this manner (v.5c)! This is indeed the pinnacle of self-destructive *peša'*, leaving God with no choice but to destroy Bethel. And in fact there must have originally followed here a mention of the punishment, as is evident from the pattern of the other oracles against Bethel (3:14 and 5:4-5). But due to the editorial addition of vv.6-11 it was relegated to v.12 where it had to be rephrased in order to accommodate its new context.

At this point I would like to draw the reader's attention to a very important matter. We are used to imagining that the historical books of the Old Testament contain a more reliable description of historical reality than we can find in the prophetic or poetic literature. But as I explained in the first volume of this series, concerning the Old Testament's historical traditions, the historical books were actually written from a later perspective. In the prophetic books, on the other hand, we can discern the original sayings of the prophets (in spite of the many editorial additions). Since these sayings are contemporary with the time of the prophet, they provide an even more accurate picture of the socio-political scene of that time. Thus, from Amos' description of cultic life in Israel we can infer the following:

1) Besides Bethel, the older and very early Israelite shrine at Gilgal[24] was still an important religious center in the time of Jeroboam II. That the mention of Gilgal is original, and not added later, can be gathered from the poetic parallelism of v.4a: "Come to Bethel, and transgress; at Gilgal, multiply transgression." We would not know of Gilgal's continuing importance from the historical books; Bethel alone is castigated for the sins of the northern kingdom in the harsh rhetoric of the Deuteronomic reform.

24. See Josh 4:19-20; 5:9-10; 9:6; 10:6-9, 15, 43; 14:6; 15:7; Judg 2:1; 3:19; 1 Sam 7:16; 10:8; 11:14-15; 13:4, 7-8, 12, 15; 15:12, 21, 33; 2 Sam 19:15, 40; 2 Kg 2:1; 4:38. While some of these texts testify more to its early political rather than religious significance, it is safe to assume that an important town whose origins went back to Joshua's day would have been the site of an important shrine from the beginning.

2) Several different kinds of cultic offerings were common in the middle of the 8th century B.C.: the sacrifice (*zebah*), the tithe (*ma'aser*), the sacrifice of thanksgiving (*todah*), and the freewill offering (*n^edabah*).

Repeated Warnings Ignored (4:6-13)

The Deuteronomistic editors of Amos' sayings needed to update his message in order to make it relevant to their Judahite contemporaries. Judah had to be told that Jerusalem might be condemned to destruction by God himself in the same way that Samaria was, or Amos' message would have had no meaning for them. We know from Jeremiah's experience that such a message delivered bluntly was not received with equanimity by Judahites![25] Moreover, Amos made it sound as if God was not even going to give his people a chance to shape up; he explained the reasons for the condemnation, but the condemnation itself was the last word, to which no appeal was possible. The Deuteronomists had no need to be quite that blunt about it. Their entire approach to reform, as expressed in Deuteronomy, was to remind people that blessings were promised as rewards for obedience and curses as punishment for disobedience; i.e., for them there was always a way out, a promise that if people would only repent, things would be better.[26]

What the Deuteronomists did in vv.6-11 was a real and effective tour de force. They highlighted the inevitability of God's punitive reaction against the *peša'* mentioned in vv.4-5 by placing it at the end of a long series of refusals to repent on the part of the people. The Deuteronomic curses were transformed into whippings meant to open their eyes and goad them into changing their ways. The editors' intention can be gathered from the way the curses and their results are listed: they beat out a crescendo from

25. See Jer 7:1-15; 26:1-19; 28:1-17.
26. See the blessings and curses in Lev 26:3-40, Deut 27:1-30:20, and the deuteronomistically formulated prayer of Solomon in 1 Kg 8:30-40.

famine (v.6) to drought (vv.7-8) to destruction of crops (v.9) and finally to destruction such as Egypt, and even Sodom and Gomorrah (v.10-11), experienced. And yet, in each case, the transgressors "did not return" to the Lord. Thus, by presenting the *peša'* of vv.4-5 as the "ultimate" sin, the Deuteronomistic editors are suggesting to their Judahite readers that their own *peša'* will not be considered just another correctable mistake but rather will be the straw that breaks the camel's back and makes them liable to God's final and irrevocable punishment.

In v.12 the expression "children of Israel" from v.5c, which refers to the northern kingdom in particular,[27] is changed into the simpler and broader term "Israel" (vv.12a, 12c) in order to include Judah. In this verse the Lord is announcing what he is about to do to his people, yet precisely what he has planned for them is not described. The intimation is quite clear that it will be an unpleasant experience, but specifically what do "thus" (v.12a) and "this" (v.12b) refer to? We can only surmise that the reference must be to the alleged destruction of the altar at Bethel by King Josiah during the Deuteronomic reform (2 Kg 23:20). In the same passage (v.17) we hear about "the tomb of the man of God who came from Judah and predicted these things which you [Josiah] have done against the altar at Bethel." His bones were spared together "with the bones of the prophet who came out of Samaria" (v.18b). These two prophets cannot possibly be anyone but Amos the Judahite and Hosea the Israelite.

Insofar as "Israel" here clearly carries the meaning of the entire people of God brought out of Egypt—i.e., the southern kingdom as well as the northern—the Deuteronomistic editors are thus inviting their contemporary Judahites to look at what happened to Bethel and expect no milder fate for Jerusalem. In the same way, the destruction of the temple of Jerusalem would be wrought by none other than

27. Often translated "people of Israel" in RSV. See 2:11; 3:1, 12; 9:7 and my comments thereon. See also Hos 1:10; 3:1; 4:1.

Israel's God himself (v.12c). This is emphasized by the cultic hymn (or portion thereof) introduced in the following v.13 and ending with the cry, "the Lord, the God of hosts, is his name!"

A Proleptic Lament (5:1-3)

The third "word" begins with a lamentation addressed to the house of Israel, recognizable as such not only by its content but also by its *qinah* poetic meter. The Hebrew word *qinah* means lamentation, and it has become a technical term for the meter commonly used by laments in Hebrew poetry. Conventional Hebrew poetry employs a pattern of double verses each containing the same number of beats, or stressed syllables; usually three, sometimes four, and rarely two. By contrast, the *qinah* has three-beat verses alternating with two-beat verses. The resulting staccato cadence renders the feeling of brokenness suitable for a dirge. An attempt to reproduce this meter in English might read as follows (stressed syllables are italicized):

> *Fal*len no *more* to *rise*
> *vir*gin *Is*rael
> For*sa*ken on *land* of *hers*
> *no sav*ior

Thus, Amos is chanting over the kingdom of Israel a funeral dirge, as if its demise had already happened. The poem clearly predicts that Israel is about to receive a mortal blow from which there will be no recovery. The striking image it evokes is that of a virgin girl struck down and utterly forsaken, bereft of friends or family. The victim's virginity here emphasizes the tragedy of the fall. In the ancient Near East where one's very existence was not only secured by, but also expressed in, one's progeny, to die without children was equivalent to annihilation. In that context, to die a virgin meant to die unmarried and without children; it meant the death not only of the individual but of the family and of the family's name—utter annihilation from the face of the earth with no one to remember or care. Such, according to Amos, will be the lot of Israel: its own God will leave it forsaken on its own territory and he will neither raise his people up nor will he let anyone else do so.

In v.3 Amos conveys the Lord's message of total destruction. As was true of 3:12, this verse is sometimes construed as implying the survival of a remnant of Israel, but such is not its intent. A city that sees the number of its inhabitants dwindle from a thousand to a hundred is no longer the same city, nor is the one whose dwellers drop in number from a hundred to ten. Either one is no longer a city, as the hundred survivors in the first and the ten in the second will witness; here again, the remainder functions as a witness to the destruction, not as a hopeful sign of rebirth.

God Cannot be Found in Israel's Sanctuaries (5:4-5)

In this oracle against Israel's official places of worship, the Lord asserts that the image of him projected by the priests of Bethel and Gilgal, and endorsed by the worshipers there, is false; and because it is false, Israelites who seek the true God must seek him in some other way. The worshipers at Bethel and Gilgal may think they ensured their God's good will, but nothing could be further from the truth. The true God is the source of life and the rock of salvation for his people. Bethel and Gilgal, on the contrary, offer nothing of the sort since they themselves are heading for exile and oblivion.

The gloss on Beersheba (v.5c) is obviously that, since it breaks the poetic inversion[28] that can be detected in the rest of v.5 without it: Bethel (v.5a), Gilgal (v.5b), Gilgal (v.5d), Bethel (v.5e).[29]

---

28. An inversion follows the pattern ABB'A' in which each letter and its correspondent refer to the same or similar item or thought. One can find a clear example in Jesus' famous saying: "For whoever would *save his life* (A) will *lose it* (B); and whoever *loses his life* (B') for my sake and the gospel's will *save it* (A')." (Mk 8:35).

29. The addition of this southernmost shrine to this verse does show, however, that it was linked to the Ephraimite traditions. See vol.1, p.36-37.

A Cultic Hymn (5:8-9)

Here again, as in the previous oracle against Bethel, the addition of a cultic hymn or portion thereof, ending with "the Lord is his name" (v.8), was felt necessary in order to emphasize that it was indeed the Lord himself who had decided to destroy his own shrines. Due to the break brought about by the insertion of vv.6-7,[30] the hymn of v.8 hangs in the air with no meaning either by itself or in connection with the preceding verse or what follows in v.10. In order to give the now independent v.8 a place within the entire message of Amos, an editor added v.9 as a relative clause depicting the Lord hurling destruction upon the strong and their fortress, i.e. upon the mighty of Samaria and their corrupt cultic cities of Bethel and Gilgal.

---

30. These verses appear to be out of place and will be considered in the following section on "The Three 'Woes'."

4

The Three "Woes" (5:7, 10-25; 6:1-14)

The first "woe" (5:7, 10-17) takes up the notion of lamentation we already saw in 5:1-2, whereas the following two (5:18-27; 6:1-7) warn of Israel's impending exile without lamenting it. Interspersed throughout are editorial additions, and a passage of oracles at the end of this section recapitulates Amos' basic message.

A Call to Repentance (5:6)

This is obviously a later addition:

1) It transforms the judgmental "seek me and live" of v.4b into an offer to repent before it is too late. Although the statement in v.4b sounds as though it too may carry a positive message of hope, it is directly linked, through "but do not seek Bethel" in v.5a, to the following v.5 that announces the sure and unconditional destruction of the Bethel shrine.

2) Except for this verse, the mention of a fire devouring a place is restricted to Amos chs.1-2 and 7:4; that is to say, it appears nowhere else in the "words" and "woes" of chs.3-6. Besides, in chs.1-2 and 7:4 the Lord always sends a fire, but never himself "breaks out" like one.

3) The other two references in Amos to the kingdom of Israel as Joseph are also clearly additions (5:15; 6:6b), and in fact this usage is extremely rare in the prophets generally.[1] The practice of calling the northern kingdom "Joseph" became common only in the exilic period, after 587 B.C.

1. The exceptions are Ezek 37:16, 19; Ob 18; Zech 10:6.

The Orphaned Beginning of the First Woe (5:7)

Although the Hebrew does not have *hoy* (woe) at the beginning of the verse, we may assume that it was present originally and marked the beginning of the first "woe." It will have been dropped when v.7 was separated from its continuation in v.10 and moved up to its present position. With the postulated "woe," the grammatical construction matches that of the second and third "woes" (5:18; 6:1), which are also followed in Hebrew by one or more participles translated periphrastically into English as "to those/him/her/you who ...".[2]

In order to render the invitation to repentance in v.6 more pertinent to the Judahite readers, it needed addressees. These were readily found in the first targets of the following "woe": those who turn justice to wormwood and cast down righteousness to the earth. Consequently, the word "*woe*" had to be dropped.

The Continuation of the First Woe (5:10)[3]

One would have expected that the editor would not simply drop the word "woe" but would transpose it to the beginning of v.10 and follow it with the participial phrases of v.12b. This may have been the case at a certain point in the transmission of the text. However, a series of additions similar to v.6 in that they exhort their addressees to repent (vv.13-15) necessitated the rephrasing of the entire passage. Nevertheless, this complex editorial work did not intend to water down the terrible punishment announced at the end of the original "woe" in vv.16-17. Quite to the contrary, it follows a masterfully planned crescendo similar to the one

---

2. This is the usual way to pronounce a "woe" throughout the Old Testament: see Is 5:8, 11, 18, 20; 10:1; 29:15; 31:1; 45:9, 10; Jer 22:13; Mic 2:1; Hab 2:6, 9, 15, 19: Zeph 3:1. One may also add Jer 23:1; Ezek 34:2; Zeph 2:5; Zech 11:17, since the Hebrew nouns *ro'eh* (shepherd/one who shepherds) and *yošeb* (inhabitant/one who inhabits) are actually participles.

3. Vv.8-9 were considered as part of the previous section.

in 4:6-11 leading up to the announcement of punishment in 4:12. In both cases the ultimate addressees are the exilic and post-exilic Judahites, and the message is that they have not obeyed the Lord in spite of his repeated appeals, and that consequently he is going to implement his threat to destroy his city and his people.[4]

V.10 is the second part of the original indictment, originally following directly after what is now v.7. It now introduces a first announcement of punishment (v.11) that has been formulated along the lines of the original announcement which comes later on, in vv.16-17. V.11 is complete and makes sense when one reads it beginning with the second word *ya'an* (because); *laken* (therefore) has been added to create a link between the two verses. The combination *laken ya'an* is obviously artificial since it is unique in the Old Testament.

Editorial Embellishments (5:11-12a)

The first part of v.11 is a short indictment taken from a longer oracle occurring later in the book (8:4-7). The second part contains a punishment similar to one found in Zeph 1:13 and Deut 28:30-33, which suggests a Deuteronomistic hand—especially when one considers that the latter passage is part of Deut 28:20-57, which we have seen to be closely related to the editorial addition in 4:6-11.

As for v.12a, in its present setting the speaker cannot be anyone other than the prophet himself. However, the word "sin" occurs only here in Amos; his preferred term is "transgression," which he employs repeatedly in the first three chapters. On the other hand, "multitude of transgressions" and "greatness of sins" are paralleled elsewhere only in Jeremiah (5:6; 30:14 and 15). And there "transgressions" is used exclusively with the notion of multitude (Jer 5:6), and "sins" with that of greatness (Jer 30:14 and

---

4. The editor's intent can be further detected in the addition of "Zion" alongside "Samaria" in 6:1. See discussion below.

15), which corresponds exactly to what we read in Amos. So v.12a looks like an editorial addition, contemporary to that of v.11, whose function is to further justify the verdict of destruction and exile set forth in v.11. Israel's transgressions and sins have exceeded the limit (2:6a), and as a result God is about to destroy it completely (2:13-16; 3:11) and send it into exile (4:3).

A Fragment of the Original "Woe" (5:12b)

The last part of the original accusation (5:7, 10, 12b) is here affixed in its original formulation as an address using the participial form.[5] It fits well with the addition in vv.11-12a because both address the perpetrators of injustice in the second person plural. The result is that the final text of vv.10-12, although heavily edited, corresponds perfectly to Amos' original message: it is the leaders' oppression of the poor and needy that calls down God's wrath upon their own nation (2:6, 13-16; 3:11; 4:2-3).

Advice and Exhortation (5:13-15)

God's judgment expressed in v.11 is final and not subject to appeal, so the only way to receive it is to keep silent. The matter is entirely in the Lord's hands. This notion of keeping silent on the day of divine reckoning appears again at the end of 6:9 and in Zeph 1:7a.[6]

Vv.14-15 return to the cautiously hopeful theme of v.6 after the break introduced by vv.8-13. By adding v.6 and dropping the word "woe" from the beginning of v.7, an editor had transformed the first "woe" from an oracle of complete and certain destruction (vv.7, 10, 16-17) into an invitation to "seek the Lord and live." But too much optimism would have clashed with the harsh words of vv.16-17. So vv.14-15 were added to represent the promised divine punishment as

5. Regarding participles in "woes" see comments above on 5:7.
6. See also Hab 2:20 and Zech 2:13.

being justified: evil brings punishment and good avoids it, as the people themselves are well aware.[7] Yes, they can reform and start to do good, but now it may be too late; there is no guarantee that doing good will definitely stay God's hand, since v.15 only suggests that "perhaps" God will be gracious. In this way vv.14-15 also confirm v.13's assertion that everything is now in God's hands.

God's Retribution Illustrated (5:16-17)

God has decided to strike, and Amos reports that decision in expressive poetry rendering God's own words via the messenger formula.[8] He paints a vivid picture of the impending catastrophe by describing not the devastation itself but rather the mournful cries of the stricken people who survive it. Constantly repeated words such as "wailing," "alas!" "mourning," and "lamentation" together drive home the depth of the tragedy to be experienced by Israel. As in 2:13-16, it is the Lord himself as commander-in-chief who will be causing such tragedy to befall his own army. And as in 3:2 and 14, an expression normally having positive connotations is used in a totally unexpected manner. The words "to pass through the midst" evoke the image of a general passing through the ranks of an army amassed to welcome him. In this case the commander is the Lord, and just when the people expect good things from him they will receive the opposite!

Warnings Against Vain Hopes (5:18-20, 27)

This second "woe" expands on the theme of positive expectations meeting with a very negative reality. The expression "day of the Lord" referred to the day of his visitation to his city as victorious leader against his and his city's enemies. Consequently, this was perceived as a bright and cheerful occasion, a day of joy for the

---

7. See "... as you have said." in v.14.

8. See comments on 1:3ff.; the saying is bracketed by "thus says the Lord" in v.16a and "says the Lord" in v.17c.

victorious deity's city. It would be gloomy only for one's defeated enemy, for whom it would be a day of mourning and lamentation. To call the day of the Lord—Israel's deity—a day of darkness for Israel would sound oxymoronic to Amos' Israelite listeners. But this is precisely the prophet's point: the Lord will definitely be victorious on his day, but the defeated foe will unexpectedly be his own people, the Israelites themselves. God is about to attack his own city and people and destroy them! Such is Amos' totally unacceptable and unbelievable (for an Israelite) message, and he warns those who still look forward to that day that they are only deluding themselves (v.18).

Nor should anyone think they might individually escape the impending destruction. This warning Amos expresses through the story of someone who escapes from two deadly encounters, finally gets home to safety, breathes a sigh of relief, and right there suffers a fatal snake bite. Destruction strikes even in the safest place imaginable—within the secure and solid walls of one's own home, which normally afford protection from the dangers outside. In the same way the Lord, the protector of Israel against its enemies, has become its worst danger and most deadly enemy! If so, then truly the day of the Lord has become a day of darkness rather than light (v.20). And the final result of that day will be exile for Israel (v.27).

Worship Without Justice is Worthless (5:21-24)

These verses apparently do originate with Amos himself but seem to come from a different context. They were probably introduced here by his disciples in order to supply an explicit indictment for the second "woe," which, in contrast to the first and third "woes," was missing that element. Several facts point in this direction:

1) The identity of the speaker changes abruptly. These are obviously God's words, yet they are not introduced with "thus says the Lord" as we would have expected after vv.18-20 where the speaker is Amos.

2) The section can easily stand alone. It is self-sufficient in that v.24 is not another statement reflecting God's rejection of Israel's cultic actions but rather an exhortation for leaders to do what is expected of them, i.e., promote justice and righteousness. This is a theme all its own, and the notion that justice and righteousness should take priority over mere cultic acts was destined to become a trademark of the prophetic teaching.[9]

3) If vv.21-24 were part of the original "woe," then v.24 would have been antithetical to the announcement of punishment in the immediately following v.27.

4) Taking into account the rest of the second "woe," one would have expected its indictment to be directed against the mere longing for the "Lord's day," against the perception of that day as an automatic divine guarantee of Israel's well-being. On the other hand, one can see that the choice to include vv.21-24 at this juncture hits the mark since the "day of the Lord" was honored through cultic festivities.

Israel's Apostasy Began Long Ago (5:25-26)

Into this expanded "woe" (vv.18-24) the Deuteronomistic editor added vv.25-26 in order to further justify the divine sentence of judgment in v.27. The idea here is that the regular, established cult of the Lord could not have been feasible during Israel's 40 years in the wilderness because the various sacrifices it prescribes require agriculture and animal farming which would have been rendered impossible by the barren land and Israel's unsettled status in it.[10] If, then, Israel was offering sacrifices, it must have been not to the Lord but to foreign deities. And the sin of apostasy is punishable with exile according to Deuteronomy (8:19-20; 29:24-28), which leads directly to the conclusion expressed in v.27.

9. See, e.g., Hos 2:11-20; 6:6; Mic 6:6-8; Is 1:12-17.
10. See further on this Jer 7:22-23.

The Third "Woe" (6:1-7)

Since Amos' message was specifically directed at Israel, the third "woe" (vv.1 and 3-7) must originally have been aimed only at the leaders of Samaria. The addition of "those who are at ease in Zion" will have been introduced later in order to apply the book's message also to the Jerusalem authorities after the Samarian ones were already history.[11] In any case, both groups—each in its own time—here found themselves denounced as corrupt. Instead of taking care of the needs of the people, especially the poor, they were indulging in self-aggrandizement by way of oppression and violence.[12] A play on words between vv.1 and 7 accentuates the contrast between their current exalted position and their future debasement: the heads *(re'šit)* of the nations will be at the head *(ro'š)* of the exiles.[13]

V.2 seems to have been added by Amos' disciples during the Assyrian expansion into the Eastern Mediterranean coastal areas. It invites the leaders of Samaria to look around and see how the neighboring kingdoms are collapsing or have already collapsed, and reminds them that Israel is in line for the same fate: it is neither more powerful than its neighbors nor so much smaller than they as to avoid Assyria's notice. In other words, v.2 predicts the fall of Samaria, confirming in this way the theme of Amos' third "woe."

Oracles against Samaria (6:8-14)

After the oracles against the nations and Israel (chs.1 and 2), the three "words" (3:1-5:5), and the three "woes" (5:6-6:7), the collection of Amos' prophecies ends with a series of his oracles—or fragments thereof—predicting the destruction of the capital city

11. Regarding this editorial updating of Amos' words, see comments on 2:4-5; 3:1.
12. See 3:9-10 and 4:1.
13. RSV translates "first" in both cases; both words come from a root meaning "head" or "beginning."

Samaria and the entire kingdom of Israel. Thus, 6:8-14 functions as a recapitulation of Amos' message.

In v.8 we have a divine oracle predicting the destruction of Samaria and in v.9 an editorial addition emphasizing the completeness of the destruction.[14]

Like 5:13, v.10 offers advice that the best way to attempt to escape God's wrath is to keep silent. While taking care of the remains of those struck dead by God's visitation, one survivor warns the others not to even mention the Lord's name, because he might hearken to the call and come again to finish off those spared the first time.

The oracle in v.11 has the same message as the one in v.8 but emphasizes that it will be the Lord himself who will lead the assault against the city; vv. 8 and 11 may well have been connected originally as parts of one oracle.

In v.12 we find two proverbial questions introducing an indictment against those who disregard justice and righteousness. The proverbs are rhetorical questions to which the obvious answer is in the negative since it is impossible for horses to run off cliffs willingly and for one in his right mind to consider plowing the sea with oxen.[15] The implication is that those in charge of justice in Israel have in fact done the impossible by turning God's justice into poison for the people and his life-bestowing righteousness into death-dealing evil.

The final two verses of ch.6 contain a complete oracle with an indictment (v.13) and an announcement of punishment (v.14). Since the indictment in its present form begins with a participle in Hebrew, it must have been truncated in order to link it to v.12b. Originally, it may well have been a "woe." The Hebrew words *lo-debar* and *karnaim* seem to be the names of two localities where Israel was victorious in battle and thus had reason to boast.

14. See 5:3b regarding the ten left in the house.
15. The same use of rhetorical questions can be seen in 3:3-6.

Amos uses an ironic play on words to convey his message that any
boasting on Israel's part is as foolish as it is unwarranted. *Lo-debar*
means "nothing"; hence the original Hebrew of v.13a sounds
thus: "You who rejoice in nothing"—which is foolish. *Karnaim* is
the dual form of *qeren* meaning horn as a symbol for strength;[16]
Israel's boasting over its capture of *karnaim* is unwarranted since
any victory is not wrought by its own strength (v.13b) but by that
of its God, the Lord of hosts. As for Israel's punishment (v.14), it
is implemented through the agency of an unnamed nation.[17]

16. See, e.g., Ps 89:17, 24; 92:10; 132:17-18; 148:13-14.
17. See comments on 3:11.

5

The Five Visions: Amos' Call (7:1-9:6)

The last chapters contain five visions, the first four structurally connected (7:1-8:3) and the fifth standing on its own (9:1-4). The reason for the division seems to be that the last one deals specifically with the temple at Bethel and so is concerned with the religious realm, whereas the first four have to do with Samaria and the nation as a whole, i.e., the political realm.

Amos 7:1-8:3 has the same function as Hos 1-3, Is 6, Jer 1, and Ezek 1:1-3:3, which are usually termed "the call of the prophet." As a group these passages share some common characteristics, but that should not be allowed to overshadow the uniqueness of each of them. As we shall see throughout this book on the prophetic traditions, each "call" has been editorialized in order to complement the content of the accompanying prophetic book. Nevertheless, looking past the editorial revisions we can still find in each of them a core of historically accurate material that reveals the prophet's own perception of himself. In other words, each "call" does bear, as it were, the personal signature of the prophet as the foundation upon which the later editorializations arose. Therefore we must read each on its own grounds, not merely plugging it into generalizations about its genre. Such an approach will eventually confirm the conclusion I arrived at in the Introduction, namely, that each prophet is ultimately *sui generis* and that one may not speak of the scriptural prophets in broad general terms of "prophetism" or "prophetic movement."

The Structure and Message of 7:1-8:3

The key features of this section are as follows:

1) The "call" is cast in the first person singular, i.e., autobiographically.

2) Amos does not embark on his mission to Israel until after the third vision.

3) The first and fourth visions are clearly connected with seasons, which means they must have taken place at certain times of the year. The first mowing of the season would be in April and the first growth after it in May; summer fruit would be at hand in September.

4) The first and second visions follow the same pattern: God sends a disaster upon the land; Amos beseeches him to forego his decision; God acquiesces. Since the first calamity is seasonal, one can safely surmise that the second is too. In this case, the most suitable time for an extensive fire devastating a large portion of the land is mid-summer. Thus, the first, second and third visions took place most probably in the same year, consecutively, and with some interval of time between them.

5) The third and fourth visions are each followed by a passage containing words spoken by Amos in accordance with the Lord's summons (7:10-17 and 8:4-14 respectively).

6) In the first two visions Amos is allowed to react to what he is shown, while each of the last two is immediately followed by the Lord's question: "Amos, what do you see?" (7:8; 8:2) The implication is that the third and fourth times around God only wanted him to report what he saw and did not want to hear any protests.

The first conclusion we can draw from these observations and directly from the text itself is that Amos was initially reluctant to carry out the mission offered him, but that his commission was forced upon him. His reluctance is stressed in the reports of the visions, while God's imposition of his will on Amos anyway is underscored in 7:14-15. This emphasis on the prophet's reluctance to undertake his assigned task is unique to the book of Amos, and it is especially interesting when one considers that Amos' initial refusal to accept his commission is said to have actually turned back God's intention twice, and in each instance for a substantial length of time![1] It is hard to imagine that such a scenario would have been developed or even accepted at a later editorial stage,[2] which makes it highly probable that this tradition originated with Amos himself.

This is understandable if one thinks of Amos as having been the first in Israel and Judah to have seen himself entrusted to proclaim not a summons to repentance, but rather a virtually unbelievable message of God's irrevocable decision (2:6) to utterly destroy his own people. Amos had to be totally convinced himself of God's determination to do what no one—including Amos himself at first—would be able to believe he would do. This was a difficult message to accept, much less proclaim: it was a warning of divine intervention that could not be backed up by any tangible evidence of that intervention outside of the words of the message itself. And yet, the message itself was intended to judge the hearers *here and now* for their culpability in the impending disaster, not just to provide an explanation to look back on after the fact.

This priority of the divine word over its fulfillment can be seen in the way the third and fourth visions are handled. Their order appears to have been reversed, since the fourth continues the chronological series begun in the first two. The "switch" between the last two visions is even more striking when one considers that

1. Jer 1:6 seems like a similar situation but the prophet's objection is dealt with immediately and does not disturb God's timetable. Jer 20:9 reflects moments of reluctance, but only *while* the prophet is carrying out his mission.
2. Especially considering that Judahite editorial circles left intact other texts where a prophet is said to have been *forbidden* to intercede for his people (Jer 7:16; 11:14; 14:11).

the prophetic activity recorded in 7:10-17 is presented as a consequence of the third vision,[3] so that the fourth vision seems to be superfluous.[4] Why then did the editor not simply follow the more logical sequence 7:1-6; 8:1-3; 7:7-17? It is not difficult to guess. After having been refused twice by Amos, the Lord decided to force his hand by informing him that no more appeals would be accepted. The third and fourth visions left Amos no choice but to carry the unpleasant message to Israel. Had the beginning of Amos' mission been delayed until both of those visions were accounted for, it would have appeared as if Amos did not immediately obey God's clear command, as if God had to give him a double push in order to get him moving. This would have been contrary to the basic understanding of Amos and his like regarding their status as God's servants bound to do his will regardless of their personal feelings about it. When God spoke, his prophet immediately and unquestioningly obeyed. Consequently, the report of Amos' activity (7:10-17) had to follow the third vision rather than wait until after the fourth. But since this report was substantially linked to the content of what was originally the fourth vision, the order of the last two visions needed to be reversed. The result is the sequence found in Amos 7:1-8:3 as it stands now.

A closer look at 7:7-17 will show that here too the text has been arranged to emphasize the immediate effect of the divine word. The report on Amos' activity in vv.10-17 does not begin by saying that Amos did actually relay the divine word given to him in v.9. Rather, the report begins with a description of Amaziah's reaction to the content of Amos' message. In other words, the text as it stands presents the Lord's words (v.9) as already having an effect on Amaziah in Bethel *before* Amos began to relay them. The implication is that it is not *Amos'* words that trigger the event but rather *the Lord's*. It is as if Amos' activity were little more than an

3. Compare 7:9 with 7:11.

4. An attempt was made to smooth out the resulting difficulty by inserting the oracle of 8:4-8 (see below).

appendix to the main story of God's pronouncement. Amos' role appears almost as passive as that of Amaziah: he is merely invited to *see* what God is *already* doing (v.8a; also 8:2a). What he sees is the divine explanation of the divine vision (vv.8b-9; also 8:2b-3); that is to say, God's word unfolding. And he could do about it as little as Amaziah—nothing but watch it unfold and, as a prophet, declare it out loud and witness to it!

The First Three Visions (7:1-9)

In all four visions it is the Lord himself who "shows" them to Amos (7:1, 4, 7; 8:1). Whatever the original nature of these experiences might have been, they are all reported in a form that underscores God's *direct* action in producing the vision. Nevertheless, one should not go to the extreme and contend that God caused actual disasters of locusts and fire to happen in order to tell Amos what he was about to do to Israel.[5] It makes no difference to our understanding of the meaning of each vision whether it was just a figment of Amos' imagination inspired by God or the thoughts came to him when he literally saw a locust or a mason or a basket of fruit, or experienced a hot, dry day.

The first two visions simply report God's intent to punish Israel, but the third gives some background to his decision. The plumb line (vv.7-8) is an instrument used by a mason to check if a wall is standing erect or tilting to one side, the implication being that Samaria has failed the test of uprightness. As a mason will bring down a wall that has not been correctly built, so the Lord will bring down Samaria and all its people with it. However, instead of depicting a mason tearing down a wall, Amos evokes the image of a commander-in-chief passing his troops in inspection ("I will never again pass by them" in v.8bβ), as he did in the first and second "woes" (5:17b, 18).

5. In two instances God would then have been setting up catastrophes to demonstrate what he eventually was going to decide not to do anyway (vv.3 and 6)!

In v.9 the third vision refers to both the religious and political realms (v.9ab, 9c), as does the fourth vision (8:2b-3a) which parallels it. This is in tune with the three "words" where both Samaria (the political capital) and Bethel (the religious center) are addressed in turn. However, here the object of God's wrath in the political arena is not the kingdom of Israel in general but specifically the ruling "house" or dynasty, the dynasty founded by Jehu.[6] That these words reflect a real focus on the king and are not just another way to say "kingdom of Israel" is shown by the fact that Amaziah perceived Amos' words as evidence of a conspiracy against Jeroboam himself (v.10) and reported to him that Amos was predicting his death by violence (v.11). Also:

1) The singling out of a specific person occurs again in Amos' oracle to Amaziah in vv.14-18. There the reference to the entire nation's exile is actually relegated to the end of v.17, *after* the description of the fate of the high priest and his family. Once again the emphasis is not on the nation as a nation but on those currently in power over it.

2) Hosea, Amos' contemporary, inaugurates his prophecy with an oracle directed specifically against the dynasty of which Jeroboam II was a member: "... I will punish the house of Jehu for the blood of Jezreel, and I will put an end to the kingdom of the house of Israel." (1:4) Like Amos 7:11, this verse links the destiny of the kingdom to the destiny of its rulers, but both are decided by the sins of the rulers.

3) In general, the prophets attributed responsibility for a nation's sins to its leaders—the priests, the seers, the elders, the princes, and especially the king.[7]

The reign of Jeroboam's son, Zechariah, lasted only six months, ending with his death in 743 B.C. at the hand of a conspirator who

6. See 2 Kg 9:1-10:28; 10:35; 13:1, 10; 14:23; 15:8-12.
7. See, for example, Am 1:4, 8, 15; 2:3; 6:1-7; *Hos 5:1; Mic 3:1-12;* Is 7:10-17; Jer *1:18;* 2:8, *26; 4:9;* 5:31; 6:13; 8:1; 13:13.

struck him down (2 Kg 15:8-10). Since not long before that Amos has been accused of *conspiracy* against the king (v.10) and had predicted his death *by the sword* (v.9), one can easily imagine that his status as a famous prophet may well have begun around that time, more than two decades prior to the fall of Samaria in 721. But if so—if much of his fame arose from fulfilled prophecies against the dynasty of Jehu—why do we not find more references to the "house of Jeroboam" outside of 7:7-17? I believe the answer lies in the fact that the encounter with Amaziah took place at the end of Amos' activity in Israel, and not at its beginning as suggested by ch.7 in its present configuration. Consider the following:

1) The nation of Israel as a whole—represented by Samaria and Bethel—was the main object of Amos' prophetic message,[8] and this can be observed even within the third vision. The divine oracle in vv.8b-9 is primarily directed against Israel, with mention of the house of Jeroboam appended to it. Although Amaziah's initial report of this to Jeroboam only alludes to the part concerning the king (v.10b), when he quotes Amos he reports the oracle in its entirety, including the words against the whole kingdom of Israel (v.11). Likewise, the immediate object of the oracle against the high priest in v.17 may be Amaziah himself, but it too ends with a prediction of exile for the entire nation.

2) The only possible outcome of the encounter mentioned in vv.10-17 would have been Amos' expulsion from Israel, or at least from the major gathering centers in Samaria and Bethel where his voice would have been heard by the public. In fact, Amaziah explicitly bans him from Bethel in v.13. Had this happened at the start of his mission it would have effectively nipped it in the bud, which is contrary to the evidence of a well-developed message that has become clear from our study of the book of Amos.

8. As noted above, there was also a focus on Jeroboam II and Amaziah as individuals, but the primary purpose of Amos' message was to condemn all Israel for its sins.

The Prophetic Word Rejected (7:10-13)

Amaziah's reaction confirms in its way what I said earlier concerning the nature of the message of Amos and other prophets like him as being inherently unbelievable and unacceptable. The refusal of his audience to accept his message is a typical characteristic of the prophet's experience, and this usually becomes plain right at the start in the description of the prophet's "call".[9] It happens this way so often one cannot avoid the conclusion that the prophetic editorial tradition intentionally underscored the unacceptability of each prophet's message. It thereby ensured that every new generation of hearers—and later readers—of those "words" would be forced to realize in the same way that God is not always what they expect him to be.

The message for us is the same as it was for the eighth century B.C. Israelites: God is about to do to *us* that which *we* consider him incapable of because *we* very well know that he simply doesn't act that way. Put otherwise, in the case of Amos' "call," we should put ourselves in the place of Amaziah, not Amos. Unless we consider ourselves to be like the one who could not accept God's word and *therefore* fell under its judgment (vv.16-17), Amos ch.7 is little more than a story in a novel, a figment of someone's imagination written down to entertain us. What's worse, it might not be just neutral entertainment but a downright evil influence, confirming our self-righteousness, slaking our thirst for revenge against those whom we perceive as God's enemies, allowing us to be God's busybodies determining his will for the people around us, etc... It is only insofar as *I* consider *myself* to be in Amaziah's position that the text of Amos ch.7—or rather, the divine word embedded in it—can reach me with the message it intended for *me*.

There are always good reasons for rejecting the divine message, though, and Amaziah's could hardly have been more logical:

9. See Is 6:9-13; Jer 1:17-19; Ezek 2:3-7.

Amos was simply out of line because Bethel was "the king's sanctuary" and "a temple of the kingdom." (v.13b) As I indicated several times in volume one, the central sanctuary of a kingdom functioned as an expression of the king's own personal authority, so the only preaching allowed there was that approved by the king and delivered by him himself, his court, his elders, his priests, or his seers. Each sanctuary had a written *torah* expressing that approved teaching. Anything to the contrary—such as predictions of the nation's destruction and exile—would amount to outright conspiracy against king and kingdom and would be punishable by same.

So Amaziah was merely fulfilling his duties as a loyal officer of the king when he attempted to silence the prophet speaking the unwelcome words. His apparent assumption that Amos was one of the cultic prophets from Judah come to seek a "job" at Bethel is understandable since usually only the officialdom was allowed to speak at public gatherings at an official shrine.[10] He dealt with the intruder accordingly: told him he wasn't hiring and attempted to send him back to Judah to make his living through prophecy there.

"I am no prophet" (7:14-15)

Did Amos become a prophet or not? At first it seems a moot question insofar as Amos and his peers—Hosea, Isaiah, Jeremiah, etc.—are designated prophets by the scriptural tradition that calls them so. However, in Amos' day, "prophet" did not have the narrow technical meaning given it later by the scriptural canon, so that meaning is irrelevant to this passage. If, then, we attempt to read these verses without any preconceived notions of what Amos "should" be saying about his status as a prophet, we are faced with the plain fact that he

10. Perhaps Amos was perceived as an outsider because his message was critical of Israel. Also, Israel at the time was at the peak of its economic prosperity, and Amaziah may have assumed that Judah was experiencing economic hardships driving its workers, including seers/prophets, to seek employment elsewhere.

vehemently denies being one of those referred to as prophets in his time and nowhere expressly says that he did become or will become one. But let us examine this question in more detail.

First of all, it is necessary to explain a quirk of the original Hebrew that makes the passage particularly difficult. Take a look in different English translations and you will find some with "I *am* no prophet" and others with "I *was* no prophet" in v.14. Obviously, the difference is critical to understanding whether Amos considered himself to have become a prophet or not. Yet the variation on such an important point is not because one of the two is an obvious mistranslation but because in this kind of sentence Hebrew contains no verb "to be" and no indication of tense. Literally the Hebrew reads: "I no prophet, and I no son of prophet." In Hebrew sentences like this, called nominal phrases, the indication of tense comes only from the context—which means the various biblical translators have evaluated that context differently. Since the two interpretations are diametrically opposed they can't both be right, and in order to choose between them one must evaluate the context for oneself.

Secondly, playing on the difference in meaning between "seer" in v.13 and "prophet" in v.14 would be futile. If Amos denies Amaziah's assumption that he is a "seer" by saying that he is not a "prophet," this is merely proof that in Amos' time these terms were interchangeable.[11] Besides, even the book's editor does not shy away from introducing Amos as having "seen"[12] the words revealed to him (1:1), which could identify him as a "seer".[13] As for the activity of the "prophet/seer" on the one hand, and that of Amos on the other, they are both referred to with the same verb "prophesy."[14]

11. See also 2 Kg 17:13; Is 29:10; Mic 3:6-7.
12. The verb *hazah* (to see) is from the same root as *hozeh* (seer), in Hebrew as in English.
13. See also *Mic 1:1;* Is 1:1; 2:1.
14. The verb *hitnabbe'* derives from the same root as *nabi'* (prophet); see vv.12-13 and v.15.

Thirdly, appealing to the fact that Amos was asked to prophesy in order to conclude that he became a prophet is in fact begging the question. Those exegetes who maintain that Amos was different from the other prophets of his time are forced to qualify their statement by adding that, although Amos became a prophet, he did not become like the others; he became "a different kind of prophet." When asked what they mean by that, they will still have to explain what Amos became, giving thus a new definition to the term "prophet" when applied to Amos. But this is at best a vicious circle. These new, specialized definitions of "prophet" are inventions of a later age, and textual evidence that they were current in Amos' day does not exist.

Thus the question remains: Did Amos become a prophet or didn't he? To answer it one would have to know whether, subsequent to his "call," he continued to function as a prophet of his day would have: that is, did he earn his living through prophecy or did he at least continue to prophesy, even if free of charge? This we will never know. All we can know is what we read in the book of Amos, and that only tells us about his activity in the kingdom of Israel for a very limited period of time. In addition it does also mention what he was before, namely, a herdsman[15] and a dresser of sycamores (v.14). Anything beyond these facts presented in the actual text of the book of Amos is at best conjecture, and at worst pure fantasy satisfying one's own wishful thinking.

As it stands, the text allows only the following conclusion: Amos the non-prophet acted as a prophet would, having been forced by the Lord to do so; and he did so *for a short period at a given time, within the boundaries of Jeroboam II's kingdom.* What became of him is totally immaterial to the picture of the scriptural Amos who *alone*, for any and all readers, can be, is, and will ever be the *historical* and thus the *real* Amos. From this perspective, which is that of the text itself, the only plausible understanding of

15. Or shepherd (*noqed*) according to 1:1.

the nominal phrase in v.14 is: I *am* no prophet, nor *am* I a son of a prophet. What Amos became is to be delineated according to the picture—one might say, icon—drawn by the book of Amos. Nowhere does the text call this Amos a prophet, and that seems intentional. It is safer then, as I indicated in the Introduction and throughout this section, to refer to Amos and the other scriptural prophets each by his own name, approaching them not generically as "prophets" but individually as each actually appears from the book bearing his name. Otherwise, we will perceive them according to an image we will have built a priori and thus force them into a mold that may not fit them at all. One may well discover that Ezekiel is not, after all, like Amos or Isaiah or Jeremiah! Each of them is what he is *according to the book known by his name,* and in these books each of them is presented within the limits in time and space of his activity as someone having been forced by the Lord to do what he did. Each is what he is in his book, and whatever appellation we might choose for him will always be bound to be defined and understood along the lines available solely in that book.

Consequently, Amos was a herdsman and a dresser of sycamores and became during his short activity in Israel the scriptural Amos. It is the latter that is of interest to us in himself, his message, and the eventual redefinition of the term "prophet" that may come about from this message itself. And if we are to call him a prophet, then it will have to be according to this redefinition which cannot possibly be formulated *a priori,* and which has little or no relevance to what he himself or his peers called him.

An Oracle Against Amaziah (7:16-17)

Amaziah's rejection of Amos' message earns him a personal oracle tailored to his own situation as the chief priest of Bethel. Besides losing his children and his land, his own priesthood will be stripped from him: his wife will become a harlot, in express violation of the divine law regarding priests (Lev 21:7, 13-15), and he himself, as a priest the "clean one" par excellence (Lev 22:1-8), will die in an unclean land (cf. Lev 22:9). And the original word of the Lord spoken by Amos concerning Israel (v.11c) will still obtain: Israel shall surely go to exile.

Fourth Vision and Attached Oracles (8:1-14)

In the Hebrew of 8:1-3 there is a play on words between *qays* (summer fruit, vv.1, 2a) and *qes* (end, v.2b). As with the other visions, the question of whether the Lord was the author of the entire vision or Amos perceived the Lord's will at the occasion of his seeing a basket of ripe summer fruit is immaterial. Moreover, the temporal link between the third and fourth visions, which I pointed out earlier, can be seen in the use of the same image of "never again passing by Israel." (7:8 and 8:2)

The fourth vision ends in 8:3, but just as the third vision had to be followed with a report on Amos' activity in order to under-score the effectiveness of God's word, for the same reason a series of oracles were appended to the fourth vision report. It is very hard to decide whether these oracles are authentic or the work of an editor, because they contain material found elsewhere in Amos. Be that as it may, the entire series is intended to express the notion of mourning inherent in the fourth vision itself.

Vv.4-6 contain an indictment against the leaders that oppress the poor and thus enrich themselves without giving any consider-ation to God's judgment. Following are three oracles which describe the divine punishment for that sin, introduced by a liturgical hymn (vv.7-8) intended to introduce God himself as the originator of the promised calamities.

The first oracle (vv.9-10) begins with a cosmic reference sim-ilar to that found in the introductory oracle (v.8) and continues with three statements expressing the highest level of mourning.

The second (vv.11-12) states that the actual punishment will be the total lack of the word of the Lord. The "word of the Lord" which will be yearned for in vain is clearly meant to be understood as Amos' own prophetic message—"hearing the words of the Lord" calls to mind the "words" of Amos in chs.3-5, and "seeking the word of the Lord" alludes to the call to seek God in 5:4-6. It will already be too late when Israel realizes that the condemning and punishing word of the Lord communicated through the words of Amos was itself—or could have been—the bearer of salvation.

Like the second, the third oracle (vv.13-14) contains an allusion to Amos' third "word" through its use of the term "virgin" (cf. 5:1-2). Apparently the editors wanted to close the section on the visions concerning Israel[16] by linking it with Amos' last "word," in order to indicate that Amos did carry out his mission to announce the destruction of Israel. At the same time they confirmed the irrevocability of God's decision to punish Israel (see 2:6) by asserting that attempts at appeal would be futile.

The Fifth Vision and a Concluding Hymn (9:1-6)

Though linked specifically to the altar of Bethel, the divine word of punishment expressed in the fifth vision (vv.1-4) is phrased in such a way that its message is addressed to the entire nation. It could not have been otherwise since this passage concludes the "call" section as well as the entire original part of the book, i.e., the part expressing Amos' message of utter and irrevocable destructive punishment.[17] The conclusion is that the Lord will pursue the exiles even in captivity in order to slay them there! The scene here is similar to the one found in the oracle against Bethel at the end of the first "word," where both Bethel and Samaria are addressed (3:13-15).[18]

16. The fifth vision deals specifically with Bethel, but still with Israel as a whole in general; see comments below.
17. See below on the later provenance of vv.7-14.
18. See opening comments on chapter three and on 3:13-15, where I indicated that the first "word" was cast in such a way as to render Amos' message in its entirety.

As in the case of the two previous oracles against Bethel, this last one is followed by a liturgical hymn (vv.5-6) identifying the Lord as an all-powerful deity well able to implement his threat.

6

An Epilogue (9:7-15)

A Transition (9:7-8)

These verses form a hinge between Amos' original message of total and irrevocable destruction and the message of hope found in the final vv.9-15. They begin by returning to the theme of chs.1-2 where the Lord appears as the God not only of Israel but also of all the surrounding nations, including Israel's arch-enemies the Philistines and the Arameans. On the one hand, Israel is like the Ethiopians, a people traditionally viewed as the farthest possible from Palestine. That is to say, Israel has become in the eyes of its own deity, Yahweh, no more nor less valuable than the most remote of nations. On the other hand, although the exodus, the birth of Israel, is unique in its own eyes—as every birth should be for the being concerned—yet it is not unique for the Lord, who was as instrumental in the birth of both the Philistines and the Arameans as he was in the birth of Israel. It is he who brings *all* peoples alike into being, and since he is thus their Father and the Master of their destinies, it is also his prerogative to bring an end to any of them. In the first part of v.8 it sounds as if he has merely decided to exercise that prerogative in Israel's case. Nevertheless, the end of the verse announces that a part of Israel will be spared, for reasons which will become clear from the following passage.

Less Than Total Destruction (9:9-10)

God's scattering his people in exile among the nations can be compared to shaking Israel with a sieve: the "pebbles" within Israel will not fall to the ground. From v.10 we learn that only the *sinners* will die by the sword, while others—the "pebbles" saved by the sieve—will not suffer that fate. In other words, these verses allow for a difference in punishment between the sinners and the non-sinners in the "sinful kingdom." Clearly this idea is incompatible with the message of Amos who prophesied total indiscriminate destruction for Israel.

This new attitude arose during the exilic period and is found in the prophecies of Jeremiah and especially Ezekiel. Together with their oracles of doom, they both expressed the hope that the same God who destroyed Judah and Jerusalem might well decide to grant the Judahite exiles in Babylon an opportunity for a new beginning. In that case a differentiation had to be drawn between those who would remain alive for that event and those who would not live to see it happen. Hence the two categories of sinners and righteous, the former destined for punishment and the latter for salvation.[1] But if this is true of Judah, it should also be true of Israel. Such thoughts gave rise to portrayals of the two kingdoms as two sisters, "wives" of the Lord; a call to conversion addressed to the long-forgotten northern kingdom of Israel; and predictions of the eventual unification of Judah and Israel into one entity—a new "Israel"—in the new messianic era.[2]

It is interesting that although the post-exilic bearers of this tradition were mainly Judahites, as evidenced by the appellation "Jews,"[3] the name of the new community is Israel. This is due to the fact that this name was originally linked with Ephraim, the tribe of the exodus and bearer of the normative tradition of the Lord. According to that tradition, the Lord is the maker of Israel, and, conversely, that which he brings to life is Israel. In other words, only the use of "Israel" could have kept the full identity between the God of exodus and the God of the "new exodus" from the Babylonian exile.

1. See, for example, Ezek 20:36-44.
2. See Jer 3:6-13, 18; Ezek 23:1-49; 37:15-28. See also Jer 31:31-34.
3. The term "Jew" is the English rendering of the Greek *Ioudaios* which translates the Hebrew *yᵉhudi* (Judahite).

Future Restoration 9:11-15

Although the new entity will be called Israel, its leader will bear the name of the *Judahite* David.[4] The reason is evident: David was the ruler under whom both kingdoms were united (2 Sam 5:1-5//1 Chr 11:1-3) and as such always remained the symbol for the ruler of God's people as a whole. Just as David established first the kingdom of Judah and then joined to it the northern kingdom of Israel, so also the new David will raise up first Judah (vv.11-12) and then Israel (vv.13-15). That vv.11-12 refer specifically to the rise of Judah can be gathered from the singling out of Edom (Judah's neighbor and enemy)[5] from all the other nations that were traditionally seen as having been under Davidic-Solomonic suzerainty.

---

4. See Jer 30:9; Ezek 34:23-24; 37:24-25.
5. See comments on the oracle against Edom in Am 1:11-12.

7

The Book of Amos and its Message

We have seen that throughout this book authentic oracles of Amos were reworked in order to preserve the original tone of his words and make them relevant for following generations. Since it was post-exilic nascent Judaism (5th-3rd century B.C.) that created the first scrolls intended to be considered as Scripture,[1] it is understandable that the last hand to edit what would become the present book of Amos came from those circles, and that the result would include a message of hope to the northern kingdom of Israel similar to the one promoted by Jeremiah and Ezekiel. Nevertheless, the final editors' faithfulness to the historical message of Amos can be seen in the fact that when they added this message of hope, they alluded to the rise of the new Judah only to introduce the new David who would be the shepherd of both Judah and Israel. And even this mention of the new David is only functional, since after it the final verses of the book do not speak of his united kingdom but rather of the northern kingdom actually addressed by Amos.[2] In other words, unlike Jeremiah and Ezekiel—or their editors—who speak ultimately of a unified Judah and Israel,[3] Amos' editors end their final version of his work with a passage concerning exclusively the northern kingdom and its future (vv.13-15), thereby remaining true to the content of his original message, which was itself addressed exclusively to that northern kingdom.

Although the canonical book of Amos ends on a note of hope, one ought to avoid the common pitfall of viewing its overall

1. See vol.1, pp.143-45.
2. That "my people Israel" in v.14 means the northern kingdom is clear from 7:8, 15; 8:2; 9:10.
3. See Jer 3:18; Ezek 37:15-28.

message as one of restoration after the calamity. It was the intention neither of Amos himself nor of his editors to make his message sound like a proclamation of "sunshine after the storm" or "light at the end of the tunnel." The fallacy of such a reading lies in the fact that it views the final verses as comprising the *ultimate* message of the book, and anything preceding them as merely a preamble to that message. In other words, it is as if the readers are already basking in the warmth of the sun and reminiscing about the storm or the experience of the tunnel; some commentators even go off the deep end and speak of the "spiritual benefit" of the calamity. At best, this is misrepresenting the text itself, since it is the message of hope that is an integral part of the message of destruction, and not vice versa, as can be seen from 9:8-10. At worst, it is misconstruing the divine word reported by Amos and his editors in this text, making it say what we want to hear rather than hearing what it really has to say.

At the time of the editing and even the canonization of the prophetic literature (between the fifth and second centuries B.C.), the so-called restoration of Judah—let alone that of Israel—was nothing more than wishful thinking or at best a hope for things to come. In other words, the book of Amos is only intended to be read by someone for whom the storm and calamity are *impending* and not in the past, be it far or immediate! After all, one begins by reading ch.1 and then the rest in order. For someone who did not go through 1:1-9:7, the following 9:8-15 does not apply. Moreover: even if someone went through the former, the latter only *might* apply, and just as easily might not, as is made crystal clear in 9:8-10. As for those who think they are already enjoying the safe haven of 9:13-15, the book of Amos can at best satisfy their curiosity about a "past" that is already *behind* them. Put otherwise, the book of Amos is not *addressed* to them, since they *cannot* possibly concern themselves with it in the same way as those who "hunger and thirst for hearing the words of the Lord, and wander from sea to sea, and from north to east, and run to and fro to seek the word of the Lord" (Am 8:11-12)—because that word is none other than his word of condemnation and judgment which they have rejected as not relevant to their situation.[4] For it is only when we perceive it and hunger and thirst for it as such that we shall have the chance to realize that as such it is also the bearer of a salvation that might apply to us. Actually, according to 9:10, those of us who already feel secure in the allegedly safe haven of 9:13-15 and who say, "Evil shall not overtake or meet us" (9:10b) sound more like "all the sinners of my people" that "shall die by the sword"! Those of us who feel secure in 9:13-15 and read—or, as it should be, hear—the book of Amos from this perspective are, after all, in the same boat as those who welcomed Amos' message because his opening statements indicted their neighbors and not them themselves.[5] By the time they realized that these opening statements were only a preamble to the real content of the "word" condemning their own misdeeds, it was already too late: they had already admitted its veracity.

Thus, the message of the book of Amos is not just to seek the Lord, not even to seek the Lord who will surely save us, but rather to seek the Lord whose word Amos proclaimed. This word (specifically, 5:6-17) tells us that this Lord, the God of hosts, did ultimately strike down his people (vv.16-17) in spite of the faint hope that he might not do so entirely (v.15b). Yet it is *this same word of condemnation* that offers an alternative: "Seek the Lord and live, lest he break out like fire in the house of Joseph and devour it, with none to quench it for Bethel...Seek good and not evil, that you may live; and so the Lord, the God of hosts, will be with you, as you have said. Hate evil, and love good, and establish justice in the gate; [and only if and when you do so] *it may be* that the Lord, the God of hosts, will be gracious to *the remnant* of Joseph." (vv.6, 14-15) And it is *this same word,* and none other, which gives us hope not only to be part of the remnant of Joseph,

4. See comments on 8:11-12.
5. See comments on the oracles against the nations in Am 1-2.

but also, when the sieve will be shaken—and it shall—to be that remnant which like pebbles will not fall upon the earth. (9:8b)

II

The Pre-Exilic Period

8

Hosea

Hosea began to prophesy around the same time as Amos but continued for a longer period. This can be gathered from several allusions to dateable events[1] and from the mention of four Judahite kings in the book's title (1:1b), compared to one for Amos.[2] We have precious little personal information about him aside from a few facts directly related to his work as a prophet. Even his birthplace, his home town, and his occupation are unknown. Like Amos, he delivered his oracles in the northern kingdom of Israel, but only from 2 Kg 23:18 can one infer that he was himself a Northerner.[3]

I shall limit my investigation to chs.1-3,[4] which constitute the

1. Hos 5:8-11 seems to allude to border skirmishes between Israel and Judah, very probably in conjunction with the Syro-Ephraimite war against Judah in the mid-730's (see further below on Is 7). The appeal to Assyria by both Israel (2 Kg 15:19-20) and Judah (2 Kg 16:7-8) and the subsequent subjugation of part of Israel by Assyria in 733 (2 Kg 15:29; 16:9) are reflected in Hos 5:13-14 (see further on Is 7-8). Hos 7:5-7 and probably 8:4 speak of palace intrigues that were a landmark of the last years in Israel when subsequent revolts saw six kings in succession between 743 and 732 (see 2 Kg 15:8-31). And in 7:11 Israel's vacillation between reliance on Egypt and reliance on Assyria for help probably refers to King Hoshea's dealings mentioned in 2 Kg 17:3-4.

2. This does not necessarily mean Hosea was active under all four kings. The list seems to be stereotypical: it occurs also in the books of Isaiah (1:1) and Micah (1:1), the two other contemporaries of Amos and Hosea. Nevertheless, the multiplicity of names compared to Uzziah alone in Amos may well reflect the editor's knowledge of Hosea's longer period of activity. The only Israelite king in this list is Jeroboam II, no doubt because the editor was a Judahite more accustomed to using the reigns of Judahite kings for dating purposes. Jeroboam's name will have been included not only because it was during his kingship that Hosea was active but also because he is the last major representative of the "house of Jehu" that is specifically addressed in Hos 1:4.

3. See comments on Am 4:6-13.

4. Although my comments are based upon the Hebrew text, I shall follow the somewhat different versification of the Septuagint because that is what the RSV uses.

"call" narrative for Hosea just as Am 7-9 does for Amos. Despite their similar functions, these passages present us with two significant differences: (a) Hosea's "call" is at the beginning rather than the end of his book, and (b) his book is entitled not "the words of Hosea" but rather "the word of the Lord that came to Hosea." These changes reflect an editorial tendency destined to become the norm in subsequent prophetic literature.[5]

Hosea's Marriage

Did Hosea actually marry a harlot as the text seems to assert, or is the story merely an allegorical means to introduce the topic of harlotry into his message? This question has been debated for centuries, and to the present day there is no scholarly consensus. In favor of the former one can adduce the fact that many prophets performed symbolic actions in order to convey more vividly the divine message.[6] But it is also quite plausible that this is a kind of parable, a fiction intended to express the fact that Israel in its entirety, including Hosea and his immediate family, is sinning and will surely receive the consequent penalty.

To attempt our own answer to this ancient question let us begin by examining the actual terminology used in the original Hebrew text. Hos 1:2 reads: "Go, take to yourself a wife of harlotry and have children of harlotry for the land commits great harlotry by forsaking the Lord." Consider the following:

1) If the author had intended to say that Gomer was in fact a prostitute, the Hebrew would have read *'iššah zonah* (a harlot woman/wife). Instead we find the unique term *'ešet zᵉnunim* (a woman/wife of harlotry).

2) Hosea's offspring, including two sons, are called "children of

---

5. See the call passages in Jer 1 and Ezek 1-3 and the titles in Joel 1:1; Mic 1:1; Zeph 1:1 as well as Jer 1:2, 3; Ezek 1:3; Hag 1:1; Zech 1:1. The relegation of Isaiah's call to ch.6 is an exception, the reason for which is explained below in the comments on Isaiah.

6. See Is 20; Jer 27-28; Ezek 4-5.

harlotry" (*zᵉnunim*). If by "person of harlotry" the author of this text meant simply "harlot," that term would have implied that all of Hosea's children were harlots, including the boys!

What, then, does "person of harlotry" mean? A review of the other instances of *zᵉnunim* in Hosea will reveal that all refer to Israel's faithless behavior toward the Lord, its predilection to abandon him and go after other gods (2:2, 4; 4:12; 5:4).[7] Can it have the same meaning when applied to Hosea's family? Yes! Hosea's wife and children were involved in "harlotry" insofar as they were part and parcel of the "harlot" nation Israel as a whole. There is, then, no need to view Hosea's marriage and begetting in allegorical terms, nor to imagine that he was forced by God into marrying a prostitute. The only things imposed upon him were the names of his children; indeed, the entire message of ch.1 revolves around the symbolic value of these names.[8]

The First Child: Punishment Decreed for the King (1:4-6)

As it stands now, the story of the birth of Hosea's first child encapsulates the entire message of ch.1 in that it foretells divine retribution for the sins of the king in particular (v.4) and Israel in general (v.5). However, v.5 is a later addition. Originally—as is clear from the name Jezreel given the child—the oracle was an announcement of punishment upon the house of Jehu for what Jehu had done in the valley of Jezreel (2 Kg 9). He had slaughtered Joram, the king of Israel, and Ahaziah, the king of Judah, and now his own dynasty was about to meet a similarly violent end.[9] The singling out of the king when the whole nation shares

7. The word "harlotry" carries the same meaning in Ezek 23:11, 29 and 2 Kg 9:22. The former two are from a prophetic book, and the latter comes from the Deuteronomistic History which is influenced by the prophetic tradition (see on this vol.1, p.79). See also Gen 38:24.

8. Similar instances are found in Is 7:14; 8:3-4.

9. His dynasty did in fact end this way (2 Kg 15:8-12); see comments on Am 7:7-9.

guilt corresponds to what we already found in Am 7:9-11. The king, as God's express representative, was the main perpetrator in a wayward nation's sin.

To the original oracle was added v.5 with its focus on the nation rather than the king. This emphasis is found in the following two birth stories (vv.6, 8-9) but has been added here in order to make the message of the first oracle all-inclusive. We saw evidence of similar editorial activity in the handling of the first "word" in Amos (ch.3).

The Second Child: Punishment Decreed for the Nation (1:6-8)

The second birth story predicts the destruction of the entire nation (v.6) and was intended to complement the first birth story with its similar prediction of an end to the dynasty of Jehu. The two are closely related:

1) The text links the two births syntactically, as if the second child's conception happened immediately upon the birth of the first: "... and she conceived and bore him a son...She conceived *again* and bore a daughter." (vv.3b, 6a) There is a significantly longer interval between the second and third children: "When she had weaned Not Pitied, she conceived and bore a son." (v.8)

2) The combination son-daughter reflects a complementarity expressing the notion of totality (i.e., "both x and y").

3) The first child is connected with the king; the second, with Israel. In reality these are but different aspects of the same thing.

One cannot escape the feeling that these two birth stories were conceived in a way similar to the double oracle against both Jeroboam and Israel in Am 7:9, 11. But within this unified pair we find an unexpected and out-of-place remark about pity being granted to Judah. V.7 is obviously a later editorial addition, not only because it constitutes an anticlimactic break in the flow between the second and third birth stories, but also because it suddenly introduces an otherwise absent interest in the southern kingdom.[10] What did the editor hope to accomplish with this interpolation? I believe it is intended to prepare for the comprehensive oracle of salvation in 1:11-2:1, where the ultimate salvation of Israel will be wrought through that of Judah. In other words, the editor wanted to introduce a hopeful note into an otherwise bleak prophecy of doom.

Be that as it may, does v.7 have in mind a specific event already known to the editor who wrote it? To take it as speaking of the return from the Babylonian exile is theoretically possible but very improbable. It would then refer to the same event alluded to in 1:11-2:1; besides the repetition, this would render superfluous the third birth story that follows in the final form of the text. Much more plausible is the interpretation that sees in it a reference to Jerusalem's deliverance from the Assyrian siege of 701 B.C. This was early on considered as having been due to God's direct intervention (2 Kg 19:32-34//Is 37:33-35).

The Third Child: The Punishment is Irrevocable (1:8-9)

In ancient times, nursing took a much longer period than it does today. 2 Macc 27:7, which reflects the situation in the second or first century B.C., mentions that a child was weaned at the age of three. Earlier, the period may well have been longer. From 1 Sam 1:22-25 it appears that when Samuel was weaned he was already old enough to be left in the care of the priests at a sanctuary. Therefore, several years elapsed between Gomer's second and third pregnancies. But the oracles proclaimed by means of these

10. Although Israel is not mentioned by name in the third birth story (v.9), the reference there too is clearly to the northern kingdom only. "Not my people" and "Not pitied" are siblings, and both are addressed as one by their brother "Jezreel" in 2:1.

last two children send essentially the same message to the same audience (Israel). Why then the lengthy period between them? Apparently it serves to underscore the ongoing nature of Israel's sin. The people are not being condemned for a few isolated misdeeds but for habitual evil from which they have not repented although they have had plenty of time to do so. Consequently, God's mind is made up, and his sentence *will* be carried out.

One may not conclude, however, that we have here an instance where one of the canonical prophets first called people to repentance before proclaiming his unconditional message of doom.[11] As is clear throughout the prophetic literature, any given prophet's "call" narrative is a unified whole whose intent is to show how and why the prophet was commissioned to preach his one message.[12] In Hosea's case, at no point do we read that he was sent out after the birth of the second child; only after the third is born do we find an outline of the *one* message that came out of his *one* "call" (2:2-17). In other words, the marriage and the three births make up the *one* experience of Hosea through which he was enlisted as God's messenger of doom. We may not consider the report on the second child as being either an invitation to repentance or even a threat of punishment in its own right. It exists only as part of a whole.

Besides, the editors of the prophetic books viewed the Lord's word as something much more powerful than a mere invitation to repentance that could easily be ignored. We already saw an example of their understanding in our study of Amos' "call" narrative: the Lord's word itself brings to pass that which it proclaims, and it is not dependent on human help to accomplish its purpose.[13]

---

11. In the Introduction I explained that all canonical prophets proclaimed the "end" right from the beginning.
12. See Is 6; Jer 1; Ezek 1:1-3:3; Am 7:1-8:3.
13. On this see also Is 55:10-11.

A Digression (1:10-2:1)

Another editorial addition. This one reflects the teaching of the exilic and post-exilic period about a new era where a renewed Israel will join a renewed Judah under the leadership of a new David.[14] But here again, as in the case of Amos 9:11-15, the editor maintains Hosea's focus on the northern kingdom of Israel: the oracle starts (1:10) and ends (1:11d-2:1) with the mention of Israel's forgiveness and renewal; and the new era itself (1:11abc) is only the necessary preamble to the salvation of "Jezreel" and his siblings "Not pitied" and "Not my people."

The Sin of Israel (2:2-13)

Under cover of the peace and prosperity of a healthy national economy, Hosea saw a real battle being waged between Yahweh and Baal over the allegiance of Israel. Even now, any economy is ultimately based on agriculture, but this was even more true of the ancient Near East. And if agriculture was so important, it was only logical if an ancient Near Eastern kingdom would give thanks to a god of agriculture. Baal fit that description better than Yahweh. Baal was known as the storm deity, i.e., of thunder and rain, and thus the fertility of the earth was his domain. The Israelites began to ask themselves an important question: who was ultimately the grantor of life and prosperity for the kingdom and its people—Baal or Yahweh? To many the answer was obvious, and they began to worship Baal in addition to, or even in place of, Yahweh. But the Yahweh who spoke through Hosea was not about to share his position as Israel's one and only God. To convince his people of their error he presented himself as the plaintiff in a lawsuit against them. The *rib* (lawsuit) is a literary device used profusely in the prophetic literature. In this case it takes the form of one filed by a husband against his unfaithful

14. See comments on Am 9:7-15.

wife.[15] Consequently, the RSV translation of *ribu* into "plead" is misleading; a more accurate rendering would be "argue" or "accuse."

Israel is portrayed as Yahweh's wife who left him in order to follow other gods, particularly Baal.[16] The theme of marriage fits perfectly here because it comes directly from the Baal cult terminology. Indeed, agriculture could be conceived as the impregnation of the earth by either seeds or rain, and this lent itself easily to sexual imagery involving the deity. Hosea declared that Israel's apparent marriage to Baal was actually a re-marriage, which involved divorce from her original husband. Even worse, it constituted outright adultery because there really was no divorce—it was still Yahweh who was giving Israel the care and sustenance it imagined it was getting from Baal. In modern terminology, the husband was paying the bills for his wife's enjoyment with her lover.

In order to put an end to this masquerade and make clear the true state of affairs, the Lord had no choice but to take Israel away from its land. So long as it stayed there, whatever God would do for the people would be perceived by them as coming from Baal.[17] A vicious cycle was established, one that could not be ended except through the elimination of its basis: the land in its role as sustainer of Israel's existence had to be taken away from it. Israel *had to* be disconnected from its land, i.e., annihilated as a kingdom through exile. That is precisely what God was communicating through his "word" ending in v.13 with "says the Lord."

Only then might Israel decide to return to the Lord as a wife

15. The question sometimes arises: if God is judge over everyone, how can he be a mere plaintiff? But let us remember that this is a literary device and that in any case the judge of the putative lawsuit is not named as someone other than God. In other words, Yahweh here plays the role of both plaintiff *and* judge; he is the judge who himself has been wronged and seeks redress of his grievance through due legal process.

16. The plural "Baals" in v.13 refers either to the many altars of that god or to his multiple manifestations.

17. Recall my comments above on the lengthy period of nursing the second child: Israel showed no sign of seeing reality for itself.

to her first husband (v.7b). And should that happen, it will not be because the Israelites will have discovered God's love and care for them, but rather because that will be the only possible way for them to continue their existence. Nothing in the text speaks of Israel's return or repentance. Actually, the entire passage lays out what God will have to do—and will do—in order to prove to Israel that he alone, and not Baal, is Israel's only God. The intent of the lawsuit and the ensuing punishment is not to call Israel to repentance nor even to ultimately save it, but rather just to make this one point. The Lord has all along been the only husband Israel has ever had, just as Hosea has all along been the only husband Gomer ever had.

In order to understand the forcefulness of this last statement it is important to realize what a husband meant to a woman in the ancient Near East. Due to her utter helplessness in that society, a woman generally needed the care and protection of either her father or elder brother or husband to survive.[18] Hence the precarious position of the widow, who needed to be defended along with the orphan and the poor, under the special care of the king and his palace and ultimately of God himself.[19] By the same token, the husband—just like the father and the older brother—was the master, the "baal,"[20] of his wife in the sense that her life was in his hands. Consequently, a wife's unfaithfulness toward her husband entailed ipso facto the connotation of *peša'* (revolt).[21] In other words, Israel's infidelity meant rebellion against God's full and exclusive authority over it. What was at stake was not Yahweh's "love" or "affection" for Israel, but rather his authority as its god, i.e., his own divinity or godhead. Israel's behavior was not just unruly or immoral, it threatened to deprive Yahweh of his very

18. See, for example, Gen 38:11.
19. See Ex 22:22; Deut 10:18; 14:29; 16:11; 24:17-21; 26:12-13; 27:19; Is 1:17, 23; 10:2; Jer 7:6; 22:3; Ezek 22:7; Zech 7:10; Ps 68:5; 94:6; 146:9; Prov 15:25.
20. See comments on 2:14-23 below.
21. See comments on Am 1-2.

status as God! A deity without a people is as ridiculous a concept as a husband without a wife, or a father without children, or a king without subjects, or a master without servants or slaves; its absurdity lies in its inherent contradiction.

A Message of Hope (2:14-23)

The authentic words of Hosea recorded in 2:2-13 promise only hard times for Israel, but here they are supplemented by another editorial addition similar in spirit to the ones in 1:7 and 1:10-2:1. This passage transforms the message of doom into one of hope (v.15b). Nevertheless, the change was clearly intended to fit well with Hosea's message, not to be a radical departure from it. It is the same wilderness of destruction and exile described in negative terms in v.12 that in vv.14-15 becomes an alluring land of thriving vineyards and corresponds to the wilderness God's people found when they escaped slavery in the exodus from Egypt!

Israel's answer to this new salvific act of the Lord will be similar to the one it gave in its "youth" after the exodus (v.15c):[22] it will acknowledge him as its God. But the ensuing relationship between God and his people will not simply be a renewal of the original one. This one will be different in that the Lord will be Israel's husband without being its "*baal*" or "master."

It is important to understand the ambiguity of this word in the original Hebrew. It can be translated "Baal," meaning the proper name of a particular ancient Near Eastern deity, or simply "master" in a general sense. The word "lord" in English is similar: "the Lord" in one context can mean God, while "the lord" in another context can designate a human ruler. In English we often use capitalization to distinguish the two meanings, but the ancient Hebrew texts of the Old Testament do not differentiate between upper case and lower case. Therefore, when English versions

22. The portrayal of Israel at the exodus as a "youth" is taken up again in 11:1.

encounter *baal*, they decide whether to translate "master" or "Baal" depending on their interpretation of what the word means in context. Not only is this determination sometimes a difficult one, but there are instances where the writer deliberately used the word ambiguously, so that any single English translation would be inadequate or misleading. Such is the case here. It is the close relationship between two meanings of one word that causes God to reject the title "master" in v.16. Because this term is so closely associated with the god Baal, its use by Israel could lead to another adulterous relationship with that false god (v.17).

So Israel will find itself in a brand new relationship with its God. And this one will be irreversible since it is sealed with a covenant ensuring Israel's harmony with all creation. As creator, God is king and rules over his world in peace (v.18b) which he ensures for all his subjects (v.18c).[23] V.19 confirms what I said earlier about the parallelism between a husband's authority over his wife and a king's—or deity's—over his people: only the king or the deity can combine righteousness and justice on the one hand with love and mercy on the other, since he is both judge and father.[24] Finally, unlike the earlier relationship, the new one will be permanent because of the permanence of God's faithfulness, that is, his faithfulness to remain forever as Israel's husband (v.20a)—and so its king and lord. It is his steadfastness which will allow Israel to know him (v.20b).

As was true of the earlier editorial expansions (1:10-2:1, vv.21-23), the editor took pains to remain faithful to Hosea's original message that dealt specifically with the northern kingdom. Hence his conclusion in vv.21-23 referring to the oracle of indictment and punishment (2:2-13) as well as to Hosea's marriage (1:2-4, 6, 8-9).

The final product of chs.1-2 presents an outline of the message of the book of Hosea as it appears in detail in chs.4-14. Indeed, the book ends on an entirely positive note in ch.14, contrasting

23. See Ps 24; 68; 93; 95-99; Ezek 34:28b; see also Is 2:2-4//Mic 4:1-3; Is 11:1-9.
24. See comments on vv.2-13.

sharply with the rest of the book but corresponding exactly to what we have in 2:14-23.[25]

Another Introduction (3:1-5)

Although some English translations have "The Lord said, 'Go again, love a woman ...'" in v.1, the adverb "again" actually applies to "said" rather than "go, love." A more accurate rendering would be: "Again the Lord said to me, 'Go, love a woman ...'" The function of "again" here is simply to connect 3:1ff. with 1:2ff., and in fact there is a clear parallel between 3:1-3 and 1:2-3.[26] But why the repetition—do these texts really report an event that happened once, and then later happened again in a remarkably similar manner?

Let us postulate that originally 3:1-3 was in the place of 1:2 so that the original "call" narrative consisted of 3:1-3; 1:3-4, 6, 8-9. In the way it presents a symbol followed by its interpretation, this passage would then be very similar to Am 7:1-9 and Am 8:1-3 which present visions followed by interpretations. To this original "call" narrative, then, the oracle found in 2:2-13 will have been attached right from the beginning. The arrangement whereby a prophet's call is immediately followed by such an oracle is a typical one and can be observed in Is 6; Jer 1:4-19; Ezek 1:1-3:21.[27] In other words, to be complete, Hosea's "call" report had to include the prophet's commissioning as well as a brief summary of the content of the message he was commissioned to proclaim. And these two parts had to correspond very closely, as is clear from the "calls" of Isaiah, Jeremiah, Ezekiel, and Amos. Consequently, because the theme of the oracle was "harlotry," that theme needed to be introduced into Hosea's "call." Specifically, because the

25. The same phenomenon is encountered in Isaiah, where ch.1 is intentionally structured so as to present in a nutshell the message of the book in its entirety.
26. The issue of the price paid for the procurement of Hosea's wife need not concern us here since it has no bearing on the wider meaning of the passage.
27. Am 7:1-8:3 is more complex but the principle is the same.

oracle mentioned a mother of harlotry (2:2) and children of harlotry (2:4), an editor formulated 1:2 to make both explicit in God's original instructions to Hosea.

What could be done with 3:1-3 then? The additions of 1:7; 1:10-2:1; and 2:14-23 made the "call" narrative quite lengthy, so it became necessary to include an introduction to the oracles contained in chs.4-14. That explains why these orphaned verses were moved to their present position. But, alone they would not be an adequate introduction for the entire message of the book of Hosea (in its final edition) because they offer no hope of final salvation for Israel.[28] Hence the addition of vv.4-5 that parallel 1:10-2:1 as well as 2:14-23. The result is that ch.3 performs two functions: on the one hand, it is part of Hosea's "call," and on the other, it introduces the following oracles.

The opening chapters of the book of Jeremiah bear a structure remarkably similar to that of Hosea. Ch.1 contains Jeremiah's "call" narrative (corresponding to Hos 1:1-2:23) followed by a brief passage in 2:1-3 (corresponding to Hos 3:1-5) introducing a long series of oracles in 2:4-6:30[29] (corresponding to Hos 4:1-14:9). The formal similarity between these two books becomes even more striking when one notices that in both cases the series of oracles begins with the same solemn address: compare "Hear the word of the Lord, O people of Israel" in Hos 4:1 with "Hear the word of the Lord, O house of Jacob, and all the families of the house of Israel" in Jer 4:4. In both cases this formula is unparalleled in the rest of the book, which indicates that it is intended as an official opening for the entire section it precedes.

---

28. See comments on 2:14-23.
29. These are interspersed with later additions, especially in ch.3.

9

Isaiah

Shortly after Amos and Hosea came and went, God called two others to the same kind of mission, this time sending his messengers to Judah rather than Israel. Micah and Isaiah seem to have been contemporaries, both of whom began to prophesy before the fall of Samaria in 722/21 B.C. Their books contain references that would not make sense after Israel had ceased to exist:

1) The title of Micah reads: "The word of the Lord that came to Micah...which he saw concerning Samaria and Jerusalem." (Mic 1:1). Moreover, the opening chapter corresponds to the title insofar as it contains two oracles, one against Samaria and Israel (vv.2-7)[1] followed by another against the kingdom of Judah (vv.8-16).

2) Although the title of Isaiah mentions only Judah and Jerusalem (1:1; 2:1), the context of Isaiah's prophecy in ch.7 is the Syro-Ephraimite war against Judah and the siege of Jerusalem, which took place under the Israelite king Pekah who reigned between 737 and 732. In addition, the book contains an oracle against Samaria in 28:1-13.

As was the case with both Amos and Hosea, Micah's oracles were edited in order to make the final form of the book end with hopeful promises of restoration (7:8-20). The final edition is definitely post-exilic, as is clear from 4:9-10.

The composition of the book of Isaiah is more complicated, in part because Isaiah himself was different from the others: he was apparently an "insider," one who was close to the inner circles of the Jerusalemite palace-temple complex. His call takes place within the temple (ch.6); he seems to have had easy access to the king himself

---

1. The reference in v.5c to Judah and Jerusalem was added later.

(7:3-17); and he consistently showed a special interest in Jerusalem, the royal family, and the kingly office.[2]

His firm trust in the Lord combined with this concern for Jerusalem emboldened him to advocate what seemed to his countrymen a politically naive rejection of all foreign military aid against foreign aggression. When it seemed clear that only Assyrian help could save Judah from the onslaught of Aram and Israel, Isaiah argued against accepting it.[3] The Lord himself, not earthly military might, would save Judah, he contended. And later, when Assyria became the aggressor, for the same reason he just as firmly opposed seeking help from either Egypt or Babylon.[4] His was not a popular stand; imagine a Pole rejecting foreign military aid in 1939, a Kuwaiti in 1990, or a Bosnian in 1993. But his success in predicting the failure of the Assyrian siege of Jerusalem, and the achievement of that "victory" over the enemy by apparently miraculous means,[5] ensured his fame throughout Jerusalem and Judah in his own day and for generations thereafter.

The key to Isaiah's popularity was not this one success but the teaching it corroborated: the inviolability and therefore permanence of Jerusalem and its temple.[6] After the fall of Samaria, Isaiah's words provided Jerusalemites with reason to believe their city would not have to suffer the same fate. And after Jerusalem did follow Samaria's example, his words offered the exiles hope that their abasement would only be temporary, that they would one day return, and their city would prosper under God's protection again. Finally, after the return, Isaiah's emphasis on the importance of the temple provided the Jerusalemite priesthood with the ammunition it needed in its fight to take over the position of leadership in the Persian province of Judah.[7]

2. See 1:21-27; 2:2-4; 3:1-26; 7:2, 13; 9:6-7; 11:1-9; 22:1-14; 29:1-10.

3. See Is 7:1-9; 8:6; see also 2 Kg 16:1-9.

4. See Is 30:1-7; 31:1-3; 39:1-8//2 Kg 20:12-19; see also Is 36:6, 9//2 Kg 18:21, 24.

5. See Is 37:5-7//2 Kg 19:5-7; Is 37:33-38//2 Kg 19:32-37.

6. See Is 2:2-4; Is 37:30-32//2 Kg 19:29-31.

7. On the priestly character of the returnee leaders, see Ezra 7:1-5; Zech 3:1-6; Hag 1:1, 12, 14; 2:2, 4, 11.

Out of deference to the memory of this great prophet who gave impetus to hope in a revived Jerusalem, his followers in Babylon and post-exilic Jerusalem, prophets and priests alike, put their oracles concerning the "new Jerusalem" under his aegis. Thus came about the extensive Isaianic literary corpus known to us as the book of Isaiah, including, besides the original words of Isaiah himself, the work of his school of thought, the "school of Isaiah."

The modern reader should not take umbrage at this phenomenon as if it were somehow dishonest. In its day this was acceptable and normal procedure and was in no way misleading; the intended readership for books of this kind would have been under no illusions as to their authorship. At a time when copyright laws were unknown, a given kind of literature, or a body of literature with a common interest, was often put under the umbrella of a single patron. Thus, David "the musician"[8] became the patron of psalmody, whose Book of Psalms includes hymns written by others;[9] and Solomon "the wise"[10] became the patron of wisdom literature such as Proverbs, Ecclesiastes, and Wisdom of Solomon, relatively little of which he personally composed.[11]

As it stands now, the book of Isaiah represents just such an amalgam of materials from different authors. It can be divided into three major parts. Chs.1-39 contain mainly oracles of Isaiah that have been expanded and edited;[12] all of the authentic sayings of Isaiah himself are to be found here. The second section, chs.40-55, comes from the latter part of the exilic period and is made up essentially of oracles spoken by an anonymous prophet of the Isaianic school toward the end of the Babylonian exile, announc-

8. See 1 Sam 16:14-23.

9. Ps 42; 44; 47-49; 50; 72; 73-83; etc.

10. See 1 Kg 3; 5:7-12.

11. For example, Prov 24:23a; 30:1a; 31:1 show unequivocally that not all of this book's sayings originated with Solomon himself. Note also that the heading "The proverbs of Solomon" occurring in 10:1 is clear evidence of editorial work, and 25:1 indicates that this work went on over a long period of time after Solomon's death.

12. Excepting chs.24-27.

ing the liberation of the Judahite exiles by the Medo-Persian king Cyrus I. Finally, chs.56-66 are comprised of oracles dealing with the situation in post-exilic Jerusalem. In order to differentiate between these three main sections, scholars refer to them as (First) Isaiah, Second Isaiah, and Third Isaiah.[13]

An Introduction to the Book of Isaiah (ch.1)

Like Hos 1-2, the material in this chapter was chosen and arranged to present in a nutshell the message of the entire book.[14] However, the emphasis is heavily on Isaiah himself as opposed to Second or Third Isaiah, in particular on his theme of indictment and punishment. The only exception is a brief oracle about a purified Jerusalem (vv.26-28) in anticipation of chs.56-66.

Structurally, ch.1 consists of two distinct sections, each beginning with the imperative "Hear ...!" (vv.2 and 10). The first contains a series of oracles culled from the entire span of Isaiah's activity up to and including the Assyrian siege of Jerusalem in 701, while the second presents itself as a single messenger speech[15] combining an indictment (vv.10-23) with an announcement of punishment (introduced with "Therefore" in v.24).

In the opening oracle of the first section (vv.2-3) Isaiah plays the role of a herald inviting two witnesses to a lawsuit initiated by the Lord against his people. But, whereas the witnesses were human in Amos (3:9), here they are "heavens and earth," i.e., the entire universe. The poetical hyperbole is warranted by the foolishness of the offense: children committing *peša*[16] *against their*

13. They are also known as Proto-Isaiah, Deutero-Isaiah, and Trito-Isaiah. This kind of nomenclature is very handy because it differentiates as well as groups together the different sections of a given biblical book. Hence, Second Zechariah refers to Zech 9-14; and Proto-Luke designates the postulated original writing at the core of what was to become our present gospel of Luke.

14. In Isaiah's case the independence of ch.1 can be even more easily detected due to the second "book title" that introduces ch.2.

15. See comments on Am 1:3ff.

16. See comments on Am 1:3ff.

own father. Even dumb beasts do not treat their masters so! The only explanation is that the Lord's people have somehow lost all knowledge and understanding.

The second oracle (v.4) follows up on this idea, first by hurling a series of disparaging epithets at the wayward people, and then by characterizing their misconduct as estrangement from God. As we shall see, the "call" of Isaiah revolves around this notion of God's holiness to which sinful man cannot draw near; hence its centrality in his message.

The third oracle (vv.5-6) states in general terms that Israel's deprivations are punishments meted out by God. This sets the stage for the fourth and last, which identifies as just such a punishment the Assyrian invasion (v.7) and subsequent siege of Jerusalem in 701 (v.8). Jerusalem would have succumbed to the same fate as the rest of Judah had the Lord not intervened (v.9).

We find in this last oracle the idea of "remnant," but here it does not bear the theological connotations it would develop in later generations. The beleaguered Jerusalem surrounded by a devastated Judah, like a lone booth in a vineyard or a lone lodge in a cucumber field (v.8), is naturally the image of a remainder or remnant. This becomes explicit with the words "a few survivors" in v.9.[17] In the same manner, Hezekiah himself calls his own besieged city a "remnant" (Is 37:4//2 Kg 19:4) in the lengthy historical narrative of the Assyrian siege of Jerusalem, and Isaiah employs the same term in his oracle (Is 37:31-32//2 Kg 19:30-31) near the end of that same narrative (Is 36-37//2 Kg 18:13-19:37). In each of these instances the word "remnant" is not a theological term but simply means "remainder," as is confirmed by the fact that it is used in this sense also to speak of Babylon, Philistia, Moab, and Damascus (Is 14:22; 14:30; 15:9; 17:3).

It is understandable, however, that the notion of "remnant" struck a responsive chord in the mind of the Jerusalemite priests

17. See also 30:17, which predicts that most of Israel will flee but some will be "left like a flagstaff on the top of a mountain, like a signal on a hill."

exiled in Babylon,[18] one which they could not resist expanding upon. Jerusalem fell at the hand of the Babylonians in 587, but out of its "remnant"—as Isaiah foretold—the Lord would initiate a fresh start.[19] The following generations of priesthood, who were the ultimate editors of the Pentateuch as well as of the Deuteronomistic History and the prophetic corpus, introduced into the Isaianic oracles the passages that adopt this theme and apply it to post-exilic Jerusalem (4:3; 10:20-22; 11:11, 16), thereby developing the meaning of "remnant" beyond the simple idea of "remainder" we find here in ch.1.

Against the background of this first section encompassing Isaiah's entire career, the second focuses on one aspect of it: his condemnation of Judah's and Jerusalem's *peša'*. With one exception noted below, these are authentic sayings of Isaiah coming from a limited time during the reign of Hezekiah, before the Assyrian siege. Their setting is either Sargon II's campaign in 711 against Ashdod to the southeast of Judah (Is 20:1) or, more likely, the perennial one of his successor Sennacherib I against the Eastern Mediterranean states.[20]

In the same vein as Amos before him,[21] but if anything even more forcefully, Isaiah criticizes a cult devoid of justice (vv.10-17). As did Amos and Hosea, he considers the ultimate evidence for the presence or absence of justice in society to be the way its leaders deal with the needy, represented especially by the widow and the orphan. By oppressing these defenseless people, Jerusalem's leaders seal the fate of their doomed city, since therein lies its *peša'*. Consequently, the true threat to Jerusalem's welfare comes

18. See on this ch.11 of vol.1.
19. Compare this to their handling of the person of Abraham; see ch.12 of vol.1.
20. See Is 8:5-8; 29:1-12 where the mention of a siege (v.3) and its sudden end (vv.5-8) seem to a refer to the event of 701 (see Is 36-39; also 2 Kg 18:13-20:19). The connection drawn between the two sections through reference to Sodom and Gomorrah (vv.9-10) argues for the latter possibility, since v.9 is part of an oracle (vv.7-9) concerning that siege (see above).
21. See Am 4:4-5.

from within, not from without; and that is why neither Egypt nor Babylon can save Judah from the Assyrian threat. The only thing that could help would be Judah's turning to the Lord in obedience (v.18); failing that, continued rebellion against him will only lead them inexorably to the slaughter (v.20). But it is a moot issue, because Jerusalem has already chosen faithlessness (v.21a): its princes are murderers (v.21b), cheats (v.22), thieves, and oppressors of the orphan and widow (v.23). Therefore, the Lord's wrath will certainly be poured out upon it (vv.24-25, 30-31).

As in Amos 9:7-10, the oracle originally announced total destruction but was reworked to differentiate between inveterate sinners (v.28) and those who would repent (v.27). The latter would lead Jerusalem back into faithfulness and righteousness (vv.26b-27; cf. v.21a). Vv.26-29 clearly represent a post-exilic addition:

1) They do not belong in the immediate context. Note that vv.30-31 continue the train of thought of vv.24-25.

2) They correspond to the message of the latter part of the book of Isaiah as expressed, for example, in chs.54; 60; 62.

3) The reference to the sacred oaks in this process of purification is telling, since elsewhere their cultic role is attacked only in much later texts such as Jeremiah (2:20; 3:6, 13; 17:2), Ezekiel (6:13; 20:28) and Third Isaiah (57:5). Compare also "garden" in 1:29b with 65:3; 66:17.

I believe this addition was triggered by the mention of the oak in v.30 as well as the characterization of Jerusalem as a harlot in contrast to its former reputation as "the faithful city" (v.21a). Hosea first employed the image of harlotry to portray the worship of deities other than Yahweh,[22] and it became common practice starting with Jeremiah and especially Ezekiel, probably under the impetus of the Deuteronomic reform's stress on exclusive worship of the Lord.[23] Consequently, the reestablishment of Jerusalem as "the faithful city"

22. See comments above on Hosea.
23. See Jer 3:1-10; 13:27; Ezek chs.16; 23; Deut 12:2-12.

(v.26b) entailed in the eyes of the post-exilic editor its rejection of any foreign cult.

And yet it is not on this positive note that the introductory chapter ends, but rather with a return to the original announcement of punishment (vv.30-31). This is a unique case in the prophetic corpus.[24] How to explain it? One solution is to consider it strictly as an introduction to the activity of Isaiah proper, whose message, as we shall see, was one of total destruction. But in this case two difficulties remain: (a) Why were vv.26-29 inserted? (b) The part of the book dedicated to Isaiah proper (chs.1-39) ends with an announcement of the Babylonian exile (ch.39)—not exactly good news for Jerusalem, but not annihilation either.

I believe the answer lies in the actual structure of the book of Isaiah. Although Third Isaiah contains two hymns to the eschatological Jerusalem (chs.60 and 62) akin to those found in Second Isaiah (51:17-52:6; 54:1-10), the third part of the book reflects an uneasy situation in post-exilic Jerusalem due to the oppression by the priestly hierarchy.[25] Actually, after the second hymn to the eschatological Jerusalem in ch.62, the tone becomes one of judgment. An appeal to God to interfere (63:7-64:12) is unexpectedly followed by oracles against his people (ch.65), the temple (66:1-4), and Jerusalem (66:5-17);[26] only thereafter comes the oracle of salvation (66:18-24). A closer look at ch.65 will even show that after first describing total destruction (vv.1-7) it suddenly shifts gears and explains that the good will not suffer that fate along with the bad (vv.8-16): they will receive the blessings of the new creation (vv.17-25) elaborated upon in 66:18-24. Thus, 1:18-29 correspond to ch.65.

24. It is true that Jer 1 and Ezek 1:1-3:21 do not include any message of restoration at all; the point here is that whenever such a positive note is struck at all, the entire edited passage concludes that way (as in Am 9 and Hos 1-3).
25. See vol.1, p.145-6.
26. Although the last oracle sounds like one of salvation, it nonetheless functions in this manner only to those oppressed by their "brothers" (v.5b). As for the oppressors, they will be "put to shame" (v.5b) as the "enemies" (v.6) of the Lord who is coming to pour out his wrath against them (vv.15-17).

On the other hand, the similarity between the situation facing Third Isaiah and that faced by Isaiah—in spite of Second Isaiah's consistently hopeful message of salvation—influenced the editor's decision to end ch.1 on a tone of warning corresponding more accurately to what Isaiah himself actually preached. The result is indeed an accurate introduction to the theme of the entire book, with special attention paid to the originator of the "school of Isaiah." The masterful work of the last editor proved to be a lasting tribute to the great Isaiah, the man of faith par excellence,[27] whose message had been essentially one of doom, and yet paradoxically included an element of hope in God's ultimate intervention to reveal himself not only as Judge, but also as Creator and Savior.

An Introduction to Chs.6-39 (chs.2-5)

After the introduction in ch.1 the book of Isaiah opens with a liturgical hymn (2:2-4) taken from the pre-exilic Jerusalemite cult.[28] The city is viewed as the center of the earth, to which all nations will flock in order to submit to Yahweh. However, this eschatological—and thus futuristic—hymn has been editorially introduced here in order to function as a background for the following chs.3-5 where Jerusalem is under divine judgment through the word of Isaiah. What Jerusalem can be and some day will be is in stark contrast to what it is at the moment. The end of the hymn invites the people to "walk in the light of the Lord" (v.5), but the immediately following section details their wickedness which shows they are not doing that (vv.6-8). Just as Amos warned the northern kingdom, now the southern one must be told that for them the traditionally bright and happy "day of the Lord" will actually prove to be a dark day of woe.[29]

27. See comments on ch.8.
28. Also found in Mic 4:1-4.
29. V.12 shows Isaiah is talking about "the day of the Lord." On the themes of darkness vs. light with respect to that day, see comments on Am 5:18-20. Explicit reference

In chs.3-5 Jerusalem is systematically castigated for every aspect of its *peša'*. The most powerful passage is the lawsuit of God against his people (5:1-7) beginning with the eloquent "song of the vineyard" (vv.1-2).[30] The forcefulness of the poem lies in the fact that no clue to its true intent is given until the last word *be'ushim* (wild, i.e., worth-less, grapes). The entire poem is designed to build up its hearers' expectations of a positive result to the hard and careful work of the husbandman—and then suddenly without warning it springs a neg-ative surprise upon them.[31] How could the Judahites who listened to it, and who were naturally familiar with the difficult life of agricul-ture, disagree that this must have been a worthless vineyard to give such poor returns to such diligent care (vv.3-6)? Then, just as they are thinking to themselves something like "put that vineyard to the torch," again comes a surprise: they themselves are the vineyard (v.7)! But by now it is too late to back down, for they themselves have already admitted the justice of God's indictment. All that remains is to await his sentence.

The entire section chs.2-5 sets the stage for God's intervention in ch.6, which explains the unusual location of the prophetic "call" in the book of Isaiah. Nevertheless, one may still wonder why the editors did not combine the call narrative with an overall introduction to the book as they did in Hosea, Jeremiah, and Ezekiel. The answer lies in the unique complexity of this book as a compilation of the works of three different "prophets" (Isaiah, Second Isaiah, and Third Isaiah). That is to say, whereas in the other cases the editors had to update the work of one person, here they were working with oracles stemming from three different periods. Moreover, the "call" of Isaiah was already integrated into a larger whole (6-9:7) similar to that found in Amos 7. On the other hand, prefacing the "call" with a section on the ills of Jerusalem (chs.2-5) may well have been the editors' device to single

to "darkness" here is in Is 5:30, which is the last verse of the entire section.

30. This was taken over by Jesus in his parable of the wicked husbandmen (Mt 21:33-46//Mk 12:1-12//Lk 20:9-19).

31. A literary device used often by the prophets. See comments on Am 1:3ff. and 3:2.

out Isaiah's activity within the larger work that deals with oracles not only of Isaiah himself but also of his "school." Their desire to set apart the work of Isaiah proper is also reflected in the inclusion of chs. 36-39, a passage that completes the section dedicated to his own words (chs.36-38) and then links it to the exile (ch.39) in order to prepare for the Second Isaianic oracles in the following chapters. In conclusion, the original Isaianic collection beginning with ch.6 probably circulated independently until it was integrated into the present book of Isaiah, at which time ch.1 was formulated in order to serve as a general introduction to the book as a whole and chs.2-5 to introduce the part on Isaiah proper.

The Call of Isaiah (ch.6)

Although kingship is dynastic, people of ancient Near Eastern kingdoms considered their reigning king to be the son of the deity in the sense that he was its direct representative.[32] This fact made the person of the king the basis for order, prosperity, and life within the realm of his kingdom.[33] Hence the belief that the absence of a king at any point in time is inconceivable, giving rise to the later traditional proclamation "The king is dead; long live the king." The herald who announces the death of the king *at the same time* declares his successor as king. The anticipation of the coronation and enthronement secures the continuous presence of kingship within the kingdom, thus ensuring that it does not even for a moment lose its basis for existence and fall prey to chaos and destruction. Given such a view of kingship, one can imagine how alarming Uzziah's leprosy (2 Kg 15:5a) must have been to his Judahite subjects, especially since this sickness "eats away" the body and in so doing gradually destroys the person himself. In Uzziah's case his weakness was such that Jotham, his son, had to administer the kingdom as his regent while Uzziah himself remained confined to his quarters (2 Kg 15:5b).

32. See Ps 2; 89:26; 2 Sam 7:14-16.
33. See Ps 72.

Isaiah saw in Uzziah's state of health a reflection of the bankruptcy of kingship itself in Judah. Therefore when Uzziah died, Isaiah did not recognize the accession of Jotham as the solution to the problem. The only possible answer in his eyes was for the Lord himself to take over the reins of kingship, and this is precisely the theme of ch.6. Isaiah saw the Lord sitting upon his throne as king (v.1a). This was nothing new in itself, since the holy of holies in a deity's sanctuary was always understood to be an earthly reflection of its heavenly throne, and the deity ruling in heaven was always called by the name of "king."[34] The novelty here lay in God's "aggressiveness":[35] this time he decided to take over personally, bypassing the mediacy of his earthly king.

Isaiah saw God overstepping the long-established boundaries assigned to him, boundaries which he himself had instituted: the train of his kingly robe was not confined to the *d^{e}bir* (the "holy of holies" or inner sanctuary) where it belonged but overflowed into the *hekal* (the "holy" or outer sanctuary; v.1b). He was personally invading an area reserved to his human servants, the priests of the royal sanctuary. His divine retinue included the *s^{e}raphim*,[36] who announced him as the "holy one" par excellence. Paradoxically, this "Holy One," whose holiness consisted in his being totally outside the human realm and unapproachable by humans, was appearing personally to Isaiah. And not just to Isaiah, for his "glory"—another way to say his "presence"[37]—extended throughout Judah, Israel, and even the entire earth (v.3).

Small wonder, then, if Isaiah felt that he as well as all Judahites were doomed (v.5), for God's holiness could never be compatible with their sinfulness. The reader should notice that Isaiah considers himself no different from his countrymen in this regard. Also of

34. See Ps 10:16; 24:8-10; 29:10; 44:4; 68:24; 74:12; 84:3; 93:1; 95:3; 98:6; 145:1.
35. See the Introduction.
36. Literally, "the burning ones" (v.2). Their specific role in the "call" of Isaiah will become clear in vv.6-7.
37. See 1 Kg 8:10-13//2 Chr 5:13-6:2. Notice also the connection there between "glory" and "cloud," which parallels that between "glory" and "smoke" in Is 6:3-4.

interest is his reference to "uncleanness of lips." This is clearly in anticipation of the role of Isaiah's lips in the following verses. Indeed, the Lord is not interested in Isaiah himself, but rather in his lips as an instrument to relay God's words verbatim. Isaiah's enthusiastic eagerness to take the commission offered him (when compared with Jeremiah's reluctance, for instance) need not impress us, as if it might reveal something about Isaiah's character. It is rather to be understood as having been forced upon him by God's anticipation, and thus circumvention, of any reluctance! What the Lord did was to make Isaiah "holy," i.e., a member of the "divine council," one of God's "holy ones."[38] We are not told why he did so. A search through the text for some suggestion of special worthiness or preparation on Isaiah's part will prove fruitless. We have here simply an unexplained decision of God—no different from his choosing Jeremiah before that prophet was even born (Jer 1:5). Isaiah realized that his induction into the divine council as a kind of "extraordinary" member had to be for a specific purpose;[39] and when the Lord asked the question of v.8a, it became clear that this was the purpose and he had no choice but to accept the charge laid upon him (v.8b).

Then came the dreadful message: "Hear and hear, but do not understand; see and see, but do not perceive." (v.9b) God did not want the Judahites nor the Israelites to change their attitude (v.10b), and Isaiah's mission was to make sure of that (v.10a). Why? "Israel does not know, my people does not understand." (1:3b) Isaiah's duty was paradoxically to make the people see, realize, understand—that they *lacked understanding*. His mission was, as it were, to take a snapshot of their situation and then show it to them. The purpose was not to convince them to change their

38. See comments on Amos 3:3-8 and Excursus there on the "divine council."
39. The alternative hardly makes sense: the Lord would have originally decided to invite Isaiah to be just a spectator at a session of the divine council, and while there he would have been moved to volunteer his services before any of the regular members had a chance to say anything!

way, *it was only to show them the justice of the Lord's decision to punish them!*[40] Isaiah was to persevere in his mission of prophecy until God was through with his mission of punishment. It would not be over until the sinful kingdom was destroyed, leaving behind it nothing more than witnesses to its annihilation (vv.11-13ab).[41]

Since v.13c represents a flagrant contradiction to the entire thrust of ch.6, it must be an editorial addition introduced here in accordance with the message of Second Isaiah and Third Isaiah. That initial impression is confirmed by the fact that the word *zera'* (seed, offspring) in the sense of the people of God (as in "offspring of Abraham") occurs only here and at 1:4 in chs.1-39, but many times in the second two parts of the book.[42] However, although this addition looks ahead to the latter part of the book, it seems also to play a role within the confines of chs.1-12:

1) The "holy *zera'* " stands in contradistinction to the "*zera'* of evildoers" condemned in 1:4 and sentenced to destruction in 6:9-10.

2) The "holiness" of this new seed must be related to the notion of holiness mentioned earlier in ch.6 and associated with Isaiah himself in vv.6-7. In ch.8 we learn that Isaiah had some disciples (v.16), that they were called his "children whom the Lord had given" him (v.18a), and that both he and they were "signs and portents in Israel from the Lord" (v.18b). Thus, "holy seed" may refer to the few who accept the message of God through Isaiah.

3) Chs.1-12 end with a series of passages whose tone is set by a messianic oracle (11:1-9)[43] that speaks of the eschatological

40. This is also the purpose of 5:1-7.
41. See comments on Am 3:12 and 5:3.
42. It is also sometimes translated "descendants" or "children." See Is 41:8; 43:5; 44:3; 45:19, 25; 48:19; 54:3; 59:21; 61;9; 65:9, 23; and especially 66:22. This last instance comes at the conclusion to the book of Isaiah and is apparently intended to correspond directly to 1:4 in the book's introduction, indicating that the latter is also the work of an editor (see above on the role of ch.1 as both introduction and epitomization of the entire book of Isaiah).
43. Notice how each of the following oracles begins with the expression "in that day" (11:10, 11; 12:1), the reference clearly being to the day on which the prophecy of 11:1-9 is

Messiah as "a shoot coming forth from the stump of Jesse" and "a branch growing out of his root." (11:1) The editor of 6:13 may well have had in mind also this text which speaks of a new ruler who will revitalize the rotten Davidic dynasty.

The Sign of Immanuel (ch.7)

The reference to "Immanuel" in Isaiah 7:10-17 is among the most famous texts in the Old Testament, but scholars have yet to reach a consensus on its meaning.[44] Nevertheless, I believe a solution to the riddle is possible when one gives serious consideration to the obviously deliberate parallelism between chapters 7 and 8. Consider the following:

1) Chs.7 and 8 each contain two oracles linked together in the same way: "And the Lord said to ..." (7:3//8:1)[45] introduces the first, while "Again the Lord spoke to ..." 7:10//8:5)[46] begins the second.

2) The first sign in each chapter is a child of Isaiah's (7:3; 8:1, 3), and both signs apply to the kingdoms of Israel and Aram.

3) In both chapters, the second sign (ch.7) or oracle (ch.8) concerns Judah. Moreover, each entails, either indirectly (ch.7) or directly (ch.8), a divine judgment against the lack of faith exhibited toward the first sign. In other words, in each chapter the second oracle is triggered by the rejection of the first.

fulfilled. The oracle in 11:10 links the word "ensign" to "root of Jesse" in 11:1, the word "ensign" appears again in 11:12, and both are directly related to the survival of the "remnant" in 11:11ff. "Remnant" is a central theme throughout chs.1-12.

44. The exceptional complexity of this passage is mirrored in the wide variety of interpretations given to it, as compared to the virtually unanimous agreement among interpreters in their understanding of the other three oracles in chs.7-8.

45. RSV has "then" in 8:1 rather than "and" but the Hebrew word it translates is the same in both instances.

46. The word order is different in the RSV translation but identical in Hebrew. The only difference is an additional word, '*od* (again) in 8:5. This is due to the fact that the addressee in ch.8 is Isaiah in both instances, whereas in ch.7 the addressees are Isaiah in 7:3 and Ahaz in 7:10. (The extra word is not reflected in the English translation because it would be redundant: "Again the Lord spoke to me again ...")

As was the case with Hosea, Isaiah's message was relayed through the symbolic names of children. His first child bore the name šᵉ'ar-yašub, which means "(only) a remnant will return." To what does this refer? Who will to return to where? Let us keep in mind that the historical background of the oracles in chs.7-8 is the Syro-Ephraimite war against Judah. Given that time frame (ca. 735 B.C.), it is hardly possible that the reference is to the return of Jerusalemites from the Babylonian exile, which didn't even begin until 587 B.C. Isaiah's purpose was to convince King Ahaz that the Lord would preserve Jerusalem from the immediate threat of Syro-Ephraimite aggression. In that situation would a divine promise that presupposed the destruction of Jerusalem 150 years later assuage King Ahaz's fears? Not likely. On the other hand, to assume that the name held out a promise of a return to Jerusalem in Ahaz' time or shortly thereafter, would mean that Isaiah was actually envisaging the destruction of the Judahite capital at the hands of the hostile alliance. But this contradicts plainly the whole drift of his words in ch.7, which is to assure Ahaz that no harm would befall Jerusalem. Thus, the only plausible meaning of šᵉ'ar-yašub is that it refers to the remnant of the Syro-Ephraimite armies that will return to their countries after failing in their attack on Jerusalem. As I pointed out in my comments on Amos 3:12 and 5:3, the remnant is not a positive sign of salvation but a negative sign of destruction, evidence that what was once whole has now been reduced to useless pieces.

Ahaz' rejection of the sign of šᵉ'ar-yašub prompted the Lord to provide yet another sign, this time to upbraid the king for his lack of faith rather than to reassure him.[47] Originally, the second sign offered by Isaiah was the following: a (Jerusalemite) woman who happens to be pregnant[48] will name her son 'immanu'el (God is with us) in

47. The link between the two signs is further evidenced by the word "again" and by an editorial addition between the two passages: "If you (pl) will not believe, surely you (pl) shall not be established" (v.9b). Although the original Isaianic address is to Ahaz and thus in the second person singular (vv.4-5), v.9b has the plural. The same shift from singular to plural is evident in vv.10-17.

48. Both *harah* (pregnant) and *yoledet* (giving birth) are participles and are linked by the

recognition of the divine intervention Ahaz didn't believe would happen—because by the time the child reaches the age of "knowledge of good and evil" (vv.14, 16)[49] the Syro-Ephraimite threat will have been neutralized. Alternatively, the reference could be in general to "women who are now pregnant," but the meaning would be the same. My interpretation takes into consideration the fact that in Hebrew the definite article followed by a singular noun is often generic, i.e., refers to everything fitting the category described by the noun. Thus, e.g., *hakk^{e}na'ani* (the Canaanite) means "the Canaanites."[50] Consequently, *ha'olmah* in v.14 may well be generic in the same way ("women" rather than "the woman"). Moreover, had the child intended by Isaiah been either his own or Ahaz', one would have expected the text to be more straightforward—especially since the immediate context (chs.7-8) explicitly mentions both Isaiah's wife and sons, on the one hand (7:3; 8:1, 3), and Ahaz himself as the addressee of the oracle, on the other.

The original oracle was reworked in the light of subsequent events. Ahaz did not heed the second sign either, and this occasioned a third sign borne by another child of Isaiah's (8:1-8). At this time Isaiah will have added the content of v.17 (which is similar to 8:5-8) to his original oracle, thus transforming it into an oracle of doom: the Assyria from which Ahaz thought to get help against the Syro-Ephraimite coalition will itself invade Judah, with devastating results. Later still, Ahaz' successor Hezekiah similarly distrusted Isaiah's reassurances (chs.36-39). Therefore, the oracle needed to be rephrased so as to include Ahaz' progeny. That is why the words of the oracle as it stands are addressed no longer to Ahaz alone but to a much larger audience, as indicated in the conjunction *w* (and), which indicates a proximate delivery.

49. This is simply a way of specifying a certain stage in one's life, most probably "the age of weaning." Weaning in the ancient Near East took place much later than it does nowadays in the Western civilizations (see 1 Sam 1:22-24; Is 11:8; 28:9). According to 2 Macc 7:27 it was done at the age of three.

50. See Gen 10:19; 12:6; 13:7; etc. Where English translations have plural "Canaanites" or "Perizzites," the Hebrew has "the Canaanite" or "the Perizzite."

switch—obvious in the original Hebrew—from the singular "you" in vv.11 and 17 to the plural "you" in vv.13-14. This larger audience is the "house of David" (v.13a), i.e., the entire palace as well as the Davidic dynasty, including specifically Hezekiah.

At a later, post-Isaiah stage, v.15 was added. As explained above, "knowledge of good and evil" was simply a phrase indicating a phase in a child's development. Here, though, it is artificially related to eating curds and honey (a child's first solid food after weaning), the idea being that "knowing good and evil" means "knowing the difference between good food and bad." Obviously, a child's ability to reject bad food comes at a much younger age than knowledge of "good and evil" in a moral sense, so the apparent purpose of v.15 is to shorten the length of time between the child's birth and the events which the following verses predict will happen when he reaches the critical age. Such a shortening of that time span will have become desirable at a later period when the birth itself of *immanu'el*, or more precisely the new-born child himself, came to function as the central content of the prophetic oracle.[51]

The end result of all of the editorial changes is what we now read in vv.10-17: an interpretation of the sign of *immanu'el* according to which it is at once good for the Lord's city, Jerusalem, and bad for the Davidic dynasty.[52] In other words, the sign of *immanu'el* was transformed into an eschatological messianic oracle in accordance with those at 9:6-7 and 11:1-9—and consequently, *immanu'el* himself became the eschatological Messiah of which the latter two oracles speak.

51. See 9:6-7; 11:1-10. I believe the intention was to make this waiting period even shorter than the one linked to the sign of *maher-šalal-haš-baz*. See comments below on 8:4.

52. The same dual meaning may be present in 8:8b, an editorial insertion which may have been intended either to conclude the preceding oracle in 8:5-8a or introduce the following editorial passage in 8:9-10. In the former case, it still refers to the Assyrian threat, and *immanu'el* at the end of the verse is meant ironically, as a sign both of God's salvation of Jerusalem and his condemnation of Ahaz. If v.8b is meant to introduce the following, then the wings are the Lord's who is viewed as the protector of Judah, in which case *immanu'el* of v.8b would have the same positive connotation as the one at the end of vv.9-10.

When the oracle was reinterpreted in this way, the birth itself of *'immanu'el* became the sign. That reinterpretation was then behind another change in the text when Greek-speaking Jews created the Septuagint translation of their scriptures beginning with the third century B.C.: the famous translation of Hebrew *ha'olmah* (the young woman) in v.14 as Greek *he parthenos* (the virgin). The virginity of the mother underscores the miraculous and thereby promotes the understanding that the eschatological king will be the result of God's direct intervention, i.e., he will not simply be another dynastic king. The related passages 9:6-7 and 11:1-9 make that same point. The first states that "to us a child is (will be) born, to us a son is (will be) given" (9:6a). The lack of a definite article, the use of the passive voice, and the declaration that what is being done is done "unto us" all suggest divine intervention.[53] As for 11:1-9, by linking the eschatological king with Jesse instead of David (v.1) it puts this promised Messiah on a par with David himself, i.e., as someone directly brought about by God and not indirectly, as through the established Davidic succession. It is this interpretation, common to all these texts in their final form, that forms the background for Matthew's use of Is 7:14 in his account of Jesus' virgin birth (Mt 1:18-25).

The Sign of Maher-šalal-haš-baz (ch.8)

Even after Isaiah offered him two "signs" reassuring him of the Lord's commitment to protect his city, Ahaz remained distrustful. What was called for after this was no longer reassurance but rather condemnation of the king for his disbelief. But how could Isaiah chastise the king without proving him wrong? And how could

---

53. This notion is not peculiar to this oracle. It is inherent in the common belief that any king upon accession to the throne becomes a "son of the deity" (Ps 2:7). Yet, I strongly believe that the context of the present oracle introduces a decisive difference: it is clearly anti-Ahaz (and anti-Hezekiah) and thus *anti-dynastic*. Even if the eschatological king is not necessarily conceived as someone who would abrogate the dynasty, he is definitely perceived as someone who would be the last in the dynasty, and thus who would "end" it, which entails "putting an end to" it. In other words, it is the *eschatological* stance of the oracle that makes the difference.

Ahaz be proven wrong until the Syro-Ephraimite threat did actually melt away without harming Jerusalem? That was still in the
future, so a new sign that would simply have condemned the king
for his distrust would have been unconvincing at best and unjust
at worst. When the time came, everyone would see if the Lord
would honor his promise—but what could be done before then?
All Isaiah could do, and what he did do, was to repeat the message
already offered twice before. The function of the *maher-šalal-ḥaš-
baz* sign in 8:1-4 is identical to that of the *šeʾar-yašub* sign: it
proclaims that the Syro-Ephraimite alliance is no threat at all to
Jerusalem. The two oracles are different, though, in that the
second emphasizes God's control of the situation:

1) Whereas Ahaz was the main addressee of both signs in ch.7,
he is curiously absent from the entire picture in ch.8.

2) Unlike the first child, the second is conceived at the express
request of the Lord (v.1). That is to say, the Lord himself is the
initiator of the sign and therefore of the event it signifies as
well—the Assyrian conquest of Aram and Israel (v.4; see also v.7).

3) The second oracle (vv.5-8) follows immediately as if it were
a continuation of the first, which it in fact is: (a) both speak of the
same invasion by Assyria, and (b) the lack of faith denounced in
v.6 is not something new but rather the original unbelieving
response of Ahaz to the sign of *šeʾar-yašub*. And in this second
oracle also the emphasis is on the Lord's direct action: "the Lord is
bringing up against them...the king of Assyria." (v.7)

One other difference between the two signs of *šeʾar-yašub* and
maher-šalal-ḥaš-baz: unlike the former, which applied strictly to
Aram and Israel, the latter includes Judah in its purview. The king
of Assyria who was going to invade Judah's enemies, Israel and
Syria, would also "sweep on into Judah" itself (v.8a).[54]

From these observations it becomes clear that Isaiah's main mes-

---

54. Note that no fourth sign precedes the fourth oracle: both the third and fourth oracles
interpret the third sign. See also in 8:14 the reference to "both houses of Israel."

sage is ch.8, to which ch.7 serves as a preamble. This conclusion is corroborated by the fact that the expression "this people" which figures prominently in Isaiah's "call" (6:9, 10) occurs elsewhere throughout chs.6-12 only here (8:6, 11, 12). Likewise, the reference to the holiness of the Lord of hosts in 8:13, and to his dwelling on Mount Zion in 8:18, hark back to Isaiah's vision in 6:1-5.[55] That is to say, ch.6 anticipates ch.8, and Isaiah's mission in ch.8 fulfills his commission in ch.6. In both instances, due to the bankruptcy of kingship, the Lord takes into his own hands the destiny of Judah.

Despite Isaiah's confidence that he was relating what the Lord would certainly do in his own time, there was no way he could prove he was right to anyone else, and in fact he was very much alone in his beliefs (vv.11-15). When he confronted Ahaz it still seemed obvious to everyone that the Syro-Ephraimite alliance was about to overpower Judah and Jerusalem. If Isaiah's position was to be proven at all, it would only be in the future, by people looking at it retrospectively. So for the time being his message had to be consigned to a more permanent medium than the spoken word: it had to become a written "word." This "testimony," entitled *l*ᵉ*maher-šalal-haš-baz* (belonging to/concerning *maher-šalal-haš-baz*), was to be bound up and sealed in the presence of two official witnesses as Isaiah's teaching left to his disciples (v.16; see v.2). After that all Isaiah could do was keep silence regarding the matter and wait in hope (v.17). In the meantime, he and his disciples would themselves function as the signs through whom the Lord of Hosts would remind the people of the message he had sent them by the hand of Isaiah (v.18).

This is the first instance where we are expressly told that a prophetic "word" was consigned to writing, i.e., as scripture. By doing so Isaiah committed not only himself but also God to that word, for better (if the Lord made good on his promise) or for

55. This is evidence that the original message of Isaiah during Ahaz' reign probably ended with 8:18; however, the oracle of 9:6-7 may also be authentic; see below.

worse (if future events proved the promise an empty one). As it turned out, his trust was not misplaced. In time the Lord fulfilled his promise and Isaiah's word was vindicated.

But would that mean that the word once vindicated as in fact the "word of God spoken to Isaiah"[56] was no longer relevant for any other purpose? No, God's word was not so lightly to be disposed of. Instead, it lived on among Isaiah's disciples, who read and accepted this "scripture" as presenting the "word of God"— yet not as a historical record of what had *already* been fulfilled in the past but rather of what was still awaiting fulfillment in the future (vv.19-20), even among generations that did not witness either the original confrontation or the original vindication.

Messianic Oracles (chs.9-12)

The oracle in 9:6-7 may have been an original part of what was "bound up and sealed" in Ahaz' time (ch.8), or it may have come from a later period, after Isaiah's confrontation with Hezekiah (chs.36-39). In either case, this oracle concerning an eschatological king would then have been the last word in the scripture that circulated among Isaiah's disciples as his "testimony."[57] Isaiah, weary of the lack of faith in the Lord exhibited by the house of David (7:13), looked ahead toward a time when the Lord would raise a worthy representative of kingship. Later, his vision found a more appropriate "home" during the exilic and post-exilic periods, when interest in the restoration of the northern kingdom also came to life.[58] At that time, 9:1-5 was introduced.

At the same time, others found cause to elaborate upon the vision of this prophet whose interest in the future of his people's kingship made him the foremost messianic prophet. Not only did

56. See 8:1, 5, 11. See also 6:8, 9, 11; 7:3, 10, 13.
57. Notice how the ending "the zeal of the Lord of hosts will do this" refers to the opening of ch.6 as well as to 8:13 and 18.
58. See further below on Ezekiel and Second Isaiah, above on Am 9:9-10. See also Jer 3:6-13, 18; Ezek 23:1-49; 37:15-28.

the editors of the Isaianic "scripture" update 9:6-7 by prefixing to it 9:1-5, but they also produced the grandiose series of messianic oracles in ch.11, with which they both extended and concluded the so-called "testimony of Isaiah" that overarches chs.6-12 in the present form of the book.[59]

59. Ch.12 contains a concluding hymn to the saving Lord, the Holy One of Israel who dwells in Jerusalem (v.6).

10

Jeremiah

The prophetic activity of Jeremiah, a priest from Anathoth, spanned the lengthy period of at least thirty years, from "the thirteenth year of Josiah's reign" (627 B.C.) until "the captivity of Jerusalem by the Babylonians" (587). To this should be added a brief period in Egypt after 587 (chs.42-44). The extended time during which Jeremiah reported God's words should not, however, be taken as an indication that he "became a prophet" in the sense that he ceased entirely to be, or function as, a priest in order to pursue a new career or hold a new office.[1] Such a conclusion would contradict the general tone of the whole book:

1) The title of the book itself divides Jeremiah's prophetic activity into at least two periods: "... to whom the word of the Lord came in the days of Josiah...and it came in the days of Jehoiakim..." (1:2, 3).

2) The impression given by the title (i.e., that Jeremiah was an ad hoc reporter of the divine word) is confirmed throughout the text, which repeatedly introduces oracles with a formula like "the word of the Lord came to him."[2]

3) Another significant feature of the title is the fact that it alone among the prophetic books refers to both the "words of the prophet" (v.1) and the "word of the Lord" (v.2). It even emphasizes the former by relegating the latter to a relative clause ("The words of Jeremiah...to whom the word of the Lord came ..."). The only other prophetic book to describe its contents as the words of

---

1. See my discussion of Am 7:14-15.
2. 1:4, 11, 13; 2:1; 11:1; 13:3, 8; 16:1; 18:5; 24:4; 28:12; 32:6; 33:1, 19, 23; 34:12; 36:27; 39:15; 49:34.

its namesake rather than the word of God is Amos. I believe this reflects the unique situation of Jeremiah in that he spoke at such varied times and settings: under Josiah (627-609), under Jehoiakim (609-597), during the first deportation to Babylon (597),[3] under Zedekiah (597-587), during the sack of Jerusalem (587), and briefly in Egypt. Given the multiplicity of occasions on which Jeremiah prophesied, the plural "words of Jeremiah" naturally seemed to warrant more emphasis than the singular "word of God."

Thus the text reflects the understanding, at least on the part of its editors, that in order to function as God's special emissary Jeremiah had to be commissioned anew each time the necessity arose. The assertion that he was chosen from his mother's womb and consecrated to this kind of life already before his birth (1:5) in no way contradicts this conclusion, since the intention of that statement is simply to underscore the fact that Jeremiah had no choice in the matter.[4]

Jeremiah's Call (ch.1)

Whereas in Isaiah's call narrative (ch.6) it is the *glory* of the Lord that forms the background of Isaiah's activity, here the *word* of the Lord takes center stage right from the beginning. It is this word that governs Jeremiah's life[5]—and begins its work already before his birth, when God pronounced his consecration as a prophet "to the nations" (v.5).

This last phrase may seem inappropriate since his mission was actually to his own country, Judah, even if it included pronouncing oracles against the nations.[6] But the reason for it may be that because Jeremiah prophesied during the fall of Jerusalem and the

3. Included in the period between Jehoiakim and Zedekiah; see 2 Kg 24:6-17.

4. See below.

5. Notice the repetition of the expression "the word of the Lord came to me" in vv.4, 11 and 13. Notice also its use in 2:1 where it is followed by Jeremiah's opening statement, "Hear the word of the Lord" (2:4).

6. Jer 25:14-38; 46-51. Notice the similar situation in Am 1-2.

concomitant collapse of Judah as an independent socio-political entity, this Judahite priest from Anathoth became a man without a country—and thus a witness for his God to the entire Near East. Direct evidence of the "universal" perspective to his prophecy may be found in his second vision: the background for the word the Lord is about to fulfill (v.12) is none other than the siege of Jerusalem (v.15) *as part of* the Babylonian sweep over the entire ancient Near East (vv.14-15).[7] In other words, the nations are right from the beginning an integral part of Jeremiah's mission; actually, according to vv.13-16, it is the Babylonian siege that will set the stage for the implementation of the Lord's word against Jerusalem.[8]

V.5 explains that this wide-ranging mission of Jeremiah's was assigned to him long before he could have any say in the matter. Such a statement is to be read in context, not as a proof text in a theological debate about issues totally foreign to it, such as free will and predestination. The verse's function is to preempt Jeremiah's attempt at getting himself out of the picture already drawn by God (v.6) when he is finally called upon to take his place in it (note the words "this day" in v.10). The point is that the matter was already settled many years beforehand and Jeremiah now has no say in it whatsoever: he shall go to whomever he is sent, he shall speak whatever he is commanded to say (v.7), and that is the end of that! In fact, such a means of forestalling any objections on his part makes sense because if he did have a choice he would certainly opt out of this particular assignment. Right from the beginning it sounds unpleasant and downright dangerous: why else would he need to be reassured that the Lord would *deliver him* (v.8)? Jeremiah here is like a soldier sent to the front line of a raging battle by his commanding officer—his will in the matter is of no account. He must simply go and do what he has to do.

7. The nations conquered and subdued by their conqueror—in this case, the Babylonians—would be forced to join his alliance and thus behave as enemies toward the peoples that were next in line on the conqueror's route. See Jer 25:13b-38 on the Babylonian sweep over the ancient Near Eastern nations.

8. See below.

That task assigned to him is to deliver a message, and as if to emphasize again that his own desires are irrelevant, he is informed that he will not even get to choose his own words. The same hand that formed him in the womb and consecrated him to be a prophet will pour God's words into his mouth (v.9). For the most part they will not be pleasant words. What makes his task a dangerous one is the fact that they will be first and foremost harbingers of destruction, and only secondarily of building up again (v.10).[9]

Since Jeremiah has no choice whatsoever, he is not given the chance, like Amos before him, to debate the matter with God.[10] He is simply invited to see what God wants him to see and report it faithfully. As was the case with Amos, the two commissioning visions are related.[11] The first (vv.11-12) is based on a play on words between *šaqed* (almond tree) and *šoqed* (watching), and informs Jeremiah that the Lord is watching over his word with the intent of "doing it," i.e., of doing what he said he would do. One notices again how Jeremiah's mission was under the aegis of the word of the Lord and controlled by it. It is as if his function is merely to act as a channel for that word.

The second vision reveals what the Lord is actually going to do. The "boiling pot, facing away from the north" (v.13) refers to the Babylonian push toward the Eastern Mediterranean (v.14). This is just the beginning; Babylon's siege of Jerusalem and Judah (v.15b) is not the ultimate purpose of God's plan but merely sets the stage for the more important conflict between Judah and Jeremiah.[12] Nevertheless, the Lord's word here is not describing background circumstances but actively creating them; the besiegers of Jerusalem will come because the Lord has called them (v.15a).

His purpose in calling them is to carry out punishment against Judah for its sins (v.16), and it is this divine judgment against

9. As is clear from the rest of ch.1.
10. See comments on Am 7:1-6.
11. Am 7:6-9; 8:1-3.
12. Described in vv.18-19; see below.

Judah that Jeremiah is to proclaim to his countrymen (v.17a). In repeating that message to them, Jeremiah is not to show any fear (v.17b);[13] if he does, then the Lord himself, not the Judahites, will give Jeremiah good cause for it (v.17c)! Why does it matter whether Jeremiah shows fear or not? Because God's city is no longer Jerusalem; "this day" Jeremiah himself has become God's city (v.18a) in order to implement the word just spoken on "this day" (v.16a)! As a city is besieged, so will Jeremiah be beset by Judahites (v.18b) who will fight against him (v.19a) due to his unwelcome message but will not prevail because the Lord himself will deliver him from them (v.19b).

The siege of Jerusalem by the Babylonians is then merely for media consumption, i.e., for those who are interested in what the camera can show. What is *really* happening—i.e., what Jeremiah's God is really interested in—is that the Lord himself is being fought against and besieged by "the kings of Judah, its princes, its priests, and the people of the land" (v.18b). The putative "people of the Lord" are in truth attacking him in his own stronghold and on his own throne, but "they shall not prevail" (v.19b). Indeed, they cannot—because now he suddenly is no longer to be located in the Holy of Holies of the Jerusalem temple! Rather, he is ensconced in his new city, Jeremiah his prophet, a city that cannot possibly be overthrown, since the uttered word is beyond the reach of even those who might destroy its originator.

The words God formerly put in the mouths of his temple priests through the established *torah*[14] are now communicated through Jeremiah's mouth. The difference between the two is that the *torah* is connected with a shrine whereas the Jeremianic word is independent of any locale and thus indestructible. Those who do not want to hear his message can "debar Jeremiah from going to the house of the Lord," but he can circumvent that by telling

13. Notice the parallel between vv.7c-8a and v.17.
14. See the Introduction.

Baruch to write down his words and go to the temple and proclaim them for him there (36:5-6). King Jehoiakim can even destroy the scroll written with Jeremiah's words (v.23), but again to no avail; upon the Lord's express orders (vv.27-28), "Jeremiah took another scroll and gave it to Baruch...who wrote on it, at the dictation of Jeremiah, *all* the words of the scroll which Jehoiakim king of Judah had burned in the fire"—and even "many similar words were added to them" (v.32). Along with those and other additions to it, Jeremiah's scroll will grow into the book of Jeremiah and will be recognized as scripture wherein the Lord is encountered through his abiding word. And it will continue to abide long after those who wanted to silence Jeremiah are dead and the temple they trusted in a pile of rubble.

God Rejects His Chosen City (ch.7)

Now that the temple is bereft of the One who was its raison d'être, the *torah* connected with it is no longer the Lord's instruction but merely the temple priests' opinion. The Lord's teaching is to be found in his new abode, Jeremiah; as of now, Jeremiah's word *is* the Lord's word. And this word solemnly warns all who blindly trust in the sanctity of the temple as a guarantee of protection that they are making a mistake (vv.1-4, 8). To ensure peace and safety for themselves, what the people should have done was to implement God's will, namely, to "truly execute justice one with another" (v.5). Instead, they oppressed the alien, the fatherless and the widow, shed innocent blood, and went after other gods (v.6; see also v.9), all the while shamelessly coming to stand before the Lord in his house, thinking he either didn't see or didn't care and would deliver them from danger anyway (v.10).

Suddenly Jeremiah drops a bombshell: God does see, and he does care, and because of the sins of his people he is prepared to do to Jerusalem what he once did to Shiloh! To understand the effect this would have on his listeners, one must realize that by the end of the 7th century B.C. Jerusalem was viewed as *the* city God had ultimately chosen to be his.[15] Shiloh, on the other hand, was a shrine of the northern kingdom of Israel, a kingdom that (in Judah's eyes) had illegally repudiated the Davidic dynasty and for its apostasy had suffered destruction and exile as divine punishment.[16] What's more, Shiloh itself had been destroyed long before that, and for the same kind of sin committed by its priests and people![17] The Judahite of Jeremiah's day would have considered Shiloh to be synonymous with apostasy, the very epitome of evil according to the Deuteronomic Reform which was in full swing at that time. Therefore, to put God's chosen city Jerusalem on a par with idolatrous, disgraced Shiloh would have been blasphemous at best. After all, for the Jerusalemite priesthood, the Lord, the God of Judah, was *by definition* the God of Jerusalem! How could they stand idly by while Jeremiah not only flatly contradicted that official theology,[18] but also in so doing suggested the inevitability of the destruction of their city? He must have sounded like a traitor to his country, and the violent reaction to his message is no different from what has been received by people considered to be traitors in all ages before and since.

Although the negative aspect of Jeremiah's message evoked this nasty response, there was a positive aspect too. He did not just reject the official theology as false, he proclaimed a different theology to be true; Jeremiah asserted that the Lord's name is what matters: he is not defined by or tied to any city but is free to make "his name" dwell wherever he chooses. His name had once dwelt in Shiloh but forsook it, once dwelled in Jerusalem but forsook it, and now dwells within his prophet Jeremiah.[19]

15. See Ps 78:67-69.
16. See 2 Kg 18:11-12.
17. See Ps 78:56-64; 1 Sam 2-3. The sins of Eli and his sons are also what occasioned God's raising up of Samuel, through whom he anointed David his chosen one (Ps 78:70-72).
18. Ps 78 constitutes a summary of this theology.
19. See above on ch.1; see also 7:12.

This is where Jeremiah diverges from the path set by the Deuteronomic Reform. The Mosaic *torah*, as updated by the reformers, circumscribed God within the world of the temple and Jerusalem, while Jeremiah's God was totally free of such limitations. Having abandoned this aspect of the official theology, Jeremiah had no choice but to abandon another: he offered no hope for escape from God's judgment. The Deuteronomistic promises of blessings for obedience and curses for disobedience always offered the people hope for the future because if they would just change their ways God would be sure to transform hard times into good times. But after publicly rejecting Jerusalem and adopting Jeremiah as his mouthpiece, the Lord could not allow Jerusalem to remain unharmed because that would have confirmed the error of all those who believed he was tied to it or defined by it. Its salvation would have proven Jeremiah wrong and the Deuteronomic Reform right in the most basic issue dividing them! So Jeremiah was not even allowed to pray or intercede for the people already marked for perdition; if he were to try, God warned that he would not listen (v.16). His verdict of total annihilation was final (v.20; also vv.27-34): Judah and Jerusalem shall join Israel and Samaria in their fate (v.34).

As if to further justify the promised destruction, the editorial passage vv.21-26 again emphasizes the incompatibility between priestly *torah* and Jeremianic *dabar* (word). From the beginning God did not require sacrifices (the temple's chief function!) but rather obedience to his voice, and his voice could always be heard from his "servants the prophets." However, if rejecting temple and *torah* paved the way for the destruction of Jerusalem, it also paved the way for post-destruction renewal. A God who was defined as the God of Jerusalem and was committed to doing everything in his power to protect it would have been a laughingstock at best after Jerusalem went up in smoke—but a God who had openly rejected that view of himself as false beforehand, and who had shown that he could take his abode wherever he pleased, could again take an active role in the life of his people after the destruction of the city that had become for them little more than an idol. And this is precisely the idea of the "new covenant" as witnessed to in Jer 31:31-34.

The Book of Consolation (chs.30-33)

The "new covenant" passage occurs in the so-called "Book of Consolation." The mainly poetic chs.30-31 constitute the original core of this material, to which were appended later the prose passages of chs.32-33. Its message of hope was originally addressed to the destroyed northern kingdom of Israel.[20] It must have been proclaimed by Jeremiah during the euphoria following the Deuteronomic reform in 621, when the decline of Assyria afforded Josiah, king of Judah, an opportunity to consider attempting to win back the territory of the former northern kingdom into his own.[21] After the catastrophe of 587, the original was reworked in order to include Judah in the promised restoration (30:3-4; 31:23-24, 27), and the entire edited passage chs.30-31 was concluded with a new oracle about the reconstruction of Jerusalem (31:38-40).

The new twist given the original prophecy of Jeremiah in the exilic and post-exilic periods can be seen also in the appended chs.32-33. They are comprised of two passages from Jeremiah's later activity in 587 (32 and 33:1-13) plus an eschatological, messianic prophecy of a reunion of Israel and Judah under the aegis of David (33:14-26).[22] The correspondence between chs.30-31 and chs.32-33 is clearly reflected in the resumption in 33:20

20. This can be gathered from the use of the names Jacob (30:7, 10, 18; 31:7, 11), Ephraim (31:6, 9, 18, 20), and Samaria (31:5), terms specific to the kingdom of Israel (see vol.1, pp.29-30). The same is true of "Rachel" in 31:15: she was the mother of Benjamin and the grandmother (through Joseph) of Manasseh and Ephraim, the main tribes of the northern kingdom (see vol.1, pp.50-51).

21. See 2 Kg 23:19-20 and 2 Chr 35:17-18; cf. Jer 31:6.

22. The express mention of Levites in conjunction with David (vv.17-18, 21-22) betrays the period of the Chronicler (see vol.1, pp.149-51).

and 25 of a theme found first in 31:35-37, i.e., that God can be relied upon to follow through on his promise of restoration.

The New Covenant (31:31-34)

At the heart of this "Book of Consolation" stands the "new covenant" passage.[23] As is true of the rest of chs.30-31, the original words of Jeremiah have been modified by later editors.[24] Originally this prophecy must have consisted of just the first 3 verses since they share common Deuteronomic themes not found in v.34:

1) The notion that God would make a new covenant with his people unlike the one he had made at the time of the exodus from Egypt (v.32), bears the stamp of Deuteronomy: "These are the words of the covenant which the Lord commanded Moses to make with the people of Israel in the Land of Moab, *besides* the covenant which he had made with them at Horeb." (29:1)[25]

2) The motif of a covenant written upon the heart (v.33b) rather than on breakable stone tablets is also Deuteronomic. Immediately after the statement from Deuteronomy quoted above we read: "And Moses summoned all Israel and said to them: 'You have seen all that the Lord did before your eyes in the land of Egypt, to Pharaoh and to all his servants and to all his land, the great trials which your eyes saw, the signs, and those great wonders; *but to this day* the Lord has *not given you a heart*[26]to under-

23. The centrality of the new covenant for the editors of the "Book of Consolation" can be seen in the reappearance of the notion of covenant in the messianic prophecy at the end of ch.33 (vv.20-21).

24. Compare v.31 and v.33 and note the addition in the former of "and the house of Judah." There was no need for a similar editing of v.33 because a modified title or first verse of an oracle is sufficient to set the tone for the rest; in this case it suggests that "Israel" in the rest of the passage embraces both Israel and Judah. Ch.30 affords another clear example of this principle: the addition in v.4 suffices for the lengthy oracle extending over 30:5-31:22.

25. Also 4;1, 44-49. See also vol.1, p.75.

26. RSV translates "mind" here, but the Hebrew word is *leb* which means literally "heart" and is the same word translated "heart" in Jer 31:33.

stand, or eyes to see, or ears to hear.' " (29:2-4) This is the reason why the original stone tablets had to be broken—together with the covenant they represented—and new ones hewn (Deut 9:1-10:5). The remedy in that case was already announced as not just new stone tablets but "a circumcision *of the heart*" (Deut 10:16), since what was required was "to serve the Lord your God with *all your heart*" (v.12). The *šʿmaʿ* of Israel, the central confession of faith of Deuteronomy,[27] proclaims the same theme: "Hear, O Israel: the Lord our God is one Lord; and you shall love the Lord your God with all your heart...*And these words which I command you this day shall be upon your heart*" (Deut 6:4-6).[28]

3) The statement "I will be their God and they shall be my people" (v.33c) as the result of the new covenant is also found in Deuteronomy: "And Moses and the Levitical priests said to all Israel, 'Keep silence and hear, O Israel: *this day you have become the people of the Lord your God.*'" (Deut 27:9-10)[29]

The original "new covenant" oracle, then, was an integral part of the entire original prophecy spanning chs.30-31, all of which Jeremiah pronounced shortly after the Deuteronomic reform. However, the original hopes linked to this new covenant were destined to be shattered. The stubborn, blind faith of the Judahites in the invincibility of their temple[30] was proven false first at the fall of Jerusalem in 597[31] and again at the second fall and final destruction of city and temple in 587. After that, Judah was not only incapable of playing the role of the heralded savior of Israel, but the southern kingdom itself was faced with exile and extinction. Consequently, the "new covenant" oracle had to be updated.

The addition of v.34 originated with Jeremiah himself some-

27. And of nascent Judaism as a whole from its earliest days. See Mk 12:29-30; also Mt 22:37//Lk 10:27.
28. See also 4:9, 29, 39; 8:2, 5; 11:13, 16, 18; 13:3; 15:7, 9, 10; 17:17, 20; 18:21; 26:16; 30:2, 6, 10, 14, 17; 32:46.
29. See further 28:9; 29:13. See also 4:20; 7:6; 14:2.
30. Jer 7:1-20; 26:1-15; 28.
31. 2 Kg 24:10-17; 2 Chr 36:10.

time after 597, most likely in conjunction with the events of 587.[32] In it he posits a paradoxical situation: a covenant under which the written *torah* is superfluous, along with any form of instruction by elders or priests in knowledge of the Lord as originator of the covenant. Everyone would spontaneously know the Lord regardless of age or social status,[33] as if the content of the divine *torah* were inborn or directly taught by God himself. What's more, the implication is that the people will not merely know the Lord's will but will actually abide by it. As the whole prior history of Israel had already shown, the two do not automatically go together; God's people had time and again fallen into sin, prompting him to implement the curse of the *torah* rather than its blessing.[34] What Jeremiah is envisaging is rather an absence of iniquity and sin, whereby only the blessing promised in the *torah* would be brought about, not the curse. The absence of sin, however, is not the outcome of people avoiding sin and succeeding in that as a result of their own effort; it is rather a humanly unattainable reality initiated by God himself. He unilaterally decides to eradicate iniquity and sin by forgiving them, i.e., by eliminating their sin from the only place where it counts—his own memory. What is no longer in his memory no longer exists.[35]

With the addition of v.34 the "new covenant" of vv.31-33 takes on a new meaning. Where a traditional covenant requires a *torah* in which people must be instructed in order to know how to

32. An exilic or post-exilic source is unlikely because of the oracle's stand against instruction. This is the essential function of the *torah*, which became a central feature of nascent Judaism (see vol.1, pp.143-4). As for the date, note that both of the added chs.32 and 33 begin with direct references to the year 587.

33. The Hebrew *qaton* can mean either little/young or little/least, and *gadol* may mean either big/old or big/great. Should the second meaning for each be intended, the idea would be that under the aegis of the new covenant there will be no need for teachers or "rabbis" who would be "greater" in matters of the Torah.

34. See Deut 28, which makes it clear that blessing and curse in the *torah* function as two sides of the same coin.

35. This explains why Paul, for whom this new covenant was implemented in and through Jesus the Christ, found it illogical that a baptized Christian would sin (Rom 6).

avoid breaking it and suffering the consequences, this one cannot be broken and offers no ill consequences. It is thus truly a "new" covenant, unlike the new covenant of the Deuteronomic Reform, which was really just a renewal of the old one. In fact, the notion of newness overpowers that of covenant, to the extent that the term "covenant" becomes equivalent to "relationship." The addition of v.34 redefines the "new covenant" of v.31 as a relationship so utterly new that it cannot possibly be compared to anything else. With this notion of utter newness we are already on our way to Ezekiel and the "new Jerusalem," Second Isaiah and the "new creation," and the "priestly" circumcision covenant granted by God as an unconditional gift.[36]

The Book of Jeremiah

The final edition of the book ascribed to Jeremiah reflects an odyssey initiated by Jeremiah himself and completed by his disciples and the post-exilic priesthood, an odyssey guided by the belief that the existence and life of the Lord's community are based solely on his word as expressed in Jeremiah's words. This can be clearly seen in both the Septuagint[37] (Greek) and Masoretic[38] (Hebrew) traditions.[39]

In the Septuagint, which seems to have kept the original order of materials in the book, the section that deals with the judgment of Jerusalem and Judah (1:1-25:13) is followed by the one

36. On Abraham and circumcision see vol.1, pp.127-33.

37. Also referred to as LXX. From Latin *Septuaginta* meaning 70, for the seventy elders who are said to have translated the Judaic sacred writings from Hebrew into Greek in Alexandria under King Ptolemy II Philadelphus (283-247 B.C.). This legend is found in the "Letter of Aristeas," a Jewish writing of the second or first century B.C.

38. Also referred to as MT (Masoretic Text) after the Masoretes who introduced the vowel signs into the consonantal Hebrew text beginning with the 8th century A.D. The name Masorete is taken from the Hebrew *Masorah*, probably meaning "tradition" and thus "traditional reading."

39. There a substantial difference in the order of the chapters in the book of Jeremiah between the LXX and the MT. The oracles against the nations (chs.46-51 of the MT and our English versions) appear in the LXX after 25:13 of the MT (and in a different order). Hence, Jer 46:1-51:64 of the MT would be 25:15-45:5 in the LXX.

addressing the nations (25:14-32:38). This is in tune with the Lord's epiphany to Jeremiah as master over the whole universe rather than over Judah only (1:5c and 10). The prophecies of restoration (33-42) are followed by the final section on the last years of Jeremiah's activity (43-51). The prominence of Baruch and especially of his writing activity in chs.43-51 may well reflect the editors' interest in relaying how Jeremiah's prophecies were kept and how they eventually became the canonical book. Ch.52 is a historical appendix corresponding to 2 Kg 24:18-25:30; in function it seems similar to the ending of 2 Kings, since it expresses hope in the permanence of the Davidic dynasty.[40]

In the Masoretic text, the first part (chs.1-25) comprises the oracles of judgment against Judah and especially Jerusalem (1-24). The last chapter in this section introduces Babylon as the scourge of the Lord against the sinful Judah (25:1-13a) as well as the other nations of the ancient Near East (25:13b-38). The third part (chs.36-45) presents the last years of Jeremiah's activity. Sandwiched between these sections is the second part (chs. 26-35) comprised of oracles of salvation and restoration culminating with the "Book of Consolation" (chs.30-34). Finally we have the oracles against the nations (chs.46-51) and the historical appendix (ch.52).

It is interesting that in both scriptural traditions the promises of restoration appear *within* the body of writings describing Jeremiah's proclamations of judgment against Judah and the people's violent rejection of his message. This seems to be the pattern for every book linked to the name of a pre-exilic prophet.[41] Its intention, I believe, is to underscore God's absolute knowledge of and power over all historical events, including future ones. This attitude was impera-tive in nascent Judaism where the Lord of Jerusalem came to be

---

40. See vol.1, p.117. See also above on Is 9 and 11 concerning the importance of David's person in exilic and post-exilic thought.

41. See comments above on Amos (5:6, 14-15; 9:8b), Hosea (1:7, 10-11; 2:1), and Isaiah (1:26-27; 4:2-6; 8:9-10; 9:1-7; 10:20-23, 24-27; 14:1-2), as well as below on Zephaniah and later on Micah.

perceived as the one, universal, omnipotent, and omniscient God:[42] the restoration of Jerusalem was not a haphazard event but rather had already been foretold and brought about by the same God who had willed and implemented its destruction. Nothing could escape the foresight of the One who said:

> "I am the Lord, who made all things, who stretched out the heavens alone, who spread out the earth—Who was with me?—who frustrates the omens of liars, and makes fools of diviners; who turns wise men back, and makes their knowledge foolish; *who confirms the word of his servant, and performs the counsels of his messengers; who says of Jerusalem, 'She shall be inhabited,' and of the cities of Judah, 'They shall be built, and I will raise up their ruins'*...I form light and create darkness, *I make weal and create woe.*" (Is 44:24-26; 45:7)

The books of Nahum, Zephaniah, and Habakkuk

The scriptural prophetic canon includes three other books whose contents are best understood against the background of the latter part of the 7th century B.C.: Nahum, Zephaniah, and Habakkuk.

Nahum's theme is the imminent fall of Nineveh, so it can be dated either to around 625 when that city was besieged by the Medes, or, more probably, to around 612 when it fell to the Medo-Babylonian coalition.

Zephaniah's title tells us that he prophesied "in the days of Josiah the son of Amon, king of Judah" (1:1b). His book castigates Judah and Jerusalem for their sins and is famous for its passage on the day of the Lord which it presents as a day of divine wrath (1:14-16). His oracles seem to have originally paralleled in form Amos 1-2. The Babylonian scourge was to overwhelm the entire universe (1:2-3); Judah's neighbors are named in 2:4-16 and Judah itself in 3:1-8.[43] But the book as it stands now splits the message against Judah and Jerusalem between a section before the

---

42. See vol.1, pp.121-6.

43. Notice how, as in Amos, the nations' punishment was a prelude to that of Judah (see 3:6-8).

oracles against the nations (1:4-2:3) and one after them (3:1-8), the latter being a preamble to the prophecies of restoration (3:9-20). Moreover, even the former section is not devoid of hope, since amid the pronouncements of total destruction, it offers a chance of escape for "the humble of the land" (2:1-3).[44] The prophecy of restoration in 3:9-20 is directly related to this hopeful note: the second pronouncement against Jerusalem is specifically directed at the leaders (3:3-4), whereas the redeemed remnant is made out of the "lowly and humble" people (3:11-13). As in the book of Jeremiah, here also God foresees, decides, and implements his will as the uncontested master of history and its events.

In Habakkuk the unnamed oppressor is either the Assyrians or, more plausibly, the Chaldeans or neo-Babylonians who followed the Assyrians as rulers of Mesopotamia and the Eastern Mediterranean coast. His oracles are similarly split into two sections, one of complaints (1:2-17) and one of curses (2:5-20), in order to include in the midst of the bad news a message of hope (2:1-4) that will find its fulfillment in ch.3. Here again, the interconnection between the promise and its realization can be seen in the fact that both 2:1-4 and 3:16-19 are cast as expressions of assuredness in patient expectation of vindication from the Lord (described in 3:3-15).

The final editions of the books attributed to Zephaniah and Habakkuk, Jeremiah's contemporaries, were patterned after that of Jeremiah for the simple reason that they too dealt with the destruction of Jerusalem. They too had to contain some reference to that city's future restoration in order that the complete message of God's past interventions and promises would be consistently conveyed to future generations.

---

44. See also the promise of restoration embedded in the end of the oracle against Philistia (2:6-7).

III

The Exilic Period

11

Ezekiel

In contrast to Jeremiah, who prophesied from within Jerusalem, his contemporary and fellow priest, Ezekiel, did so from distant Babylonia.[1] He was the first Judahite or Israelite prophet whose mission ran its course entirely outside his homeland. As a relatively high-ranking priest,[2] he must have counted among the "palace officials" deported to Babylon after the first fall of Jerusalem in 597,[3] and he began to prophesy after that. His absence from Jerusalem at the time of its final destruction ten years later explains why that event did not put an end to his work as it did to Jeremiah's. In fact, it was Ezekiel's honored status as a leading Jerusalemite priest *after* the destruction of the Lord's temple and city, that helped make him influential in the shaping of nascent Judaism's concept of God.[4]

The book begins with the spirit of the universal God (ch.1) entering into his priest Ezekiel (2:2; 3:24) and transforming him into a watchman over Israel (3:16-21) by making him ingest God's written word (3:1-3). The divine epiphany takes place outside Jerusalem and Judah, at the banks of the river Chebar in Babylonia (1:3; 3:15, 23). Being the only God of the whole world, he is able to appear here—*outside* his and his people's land—and he can speak with authority, not just about Judah

1. See 1:1, 3; 3:15, 23; 10:15, 20; 22; 43:3.
2. Note that his counsel was sought by the elders of the Judahite exiles in Babylonia (8:1; 14:1; 20:1).
3. The fact that Jerusalem was still alive and well during the earlier part of Ezekiel's activity (chs.1-24) indicates he was in Babylon before 587, and he could only have gotten there as one of the deportees of 597. See 2 Kg 24:10-17, which explains that Nebuchadnezzar's action was aimed at both the king's house and the temple (v.13), suggesting that important temple personnel would have been exiled along with civil officials.
4. See vol.1, pp.125-6.

(chs.4-24) but about all the nations (chs.25-32). As for the content of his speech, it is an announcement of the end of his "old" order (chs.33-36) in order to establish once and for all an eternal "new" one (chs.37-39) based on a "new" covenant (37:26) to be expressed in a "new" *torah* (chs.40-48).[5]

God's Universality

The idea that God has abandoned Jerusalem to take up residence in his prophet, which we already saw in Jeremiah, becomes a central theme in Ezekiel. On the one hand, Ezekiel carried out his role as the Lord's messenger while living far from Jerusalem, the clear implication being that not only the temple but even the whole of Jerusalem had been abandoned by its deity even *before* the city's collapse.[6] This emphasized the Lord's independence from his city even more powerfully than Jeremiah could do since he, after all, remained within the city until its downfall. On the other hand, if the prophetic word in which the Lord himself subsisted was contained in a scroll that Ezekiel ate (3:1-3), then the Lord himself actually became an integral part of not only the prophet's mouth and the words spoken by it, but also of his very being. Hence the repeated instances throughout the book where Ezekiel "acts out" God's word in addition to proclaiming it verbally.[7]

One might have expected the Lord's mobility to be restricted by Ezekiel's, once he, through his scrollbound word, made Ezekiel his home. But instead the effect was reversed: divine freedom of movement was granted to Ezekiel as the *ruah* (spirit) of the Lord repeatedly "picked him up," instantly transporting him over great distances![8]

5. That the "call" of Ezekiel already looks ahead to the message of chs.33-48 is shown by the fact that the theme of Ezekiel as watchman is taken up again at the beginning of ch.33 (vv.6-9; cf. 3:16-21).

6. See 10:18-22 and 11:22-25 where God's glory, expression of his presence among his people, leaves its abode in the holy of holies and ultimately settles outside Jerusalem.

7. See 3:24-5:4; 6:11; ch.8, especially v.8; 12:1-7; 21:2, 6, 11-12, 18-20; 24:15-18.

8. See 3:12, 14; 8:3; 11:1, 24; 37:1; 43:5.

This spirit plays a central role throughout the book of Ezekiel, in contrast to Jeremiah, where the divine *dabar* (word) occupied center stage. Yet the one does not replace the other; rather, the two are inextricably intertwined: "And he said to me, 'Son of man, stand upon your feet, and I will speak with you.' And when he *spoke* to me, the *spirit* entered into me and set me upon my feet; and I heard him speaking to me." (2:1-2) The content of the "spirited/spirit-borne/inspired" message is none other than the content of the "word" of the scroll which also "entered into" him (3:3).[9] In other words, the spirit within Ezekiel is not only his personal "chariot" whisking him around from place to place but is also the "chariot" of God's word, the means by which the divine message is conveyed to him.[10] And since the same spirit is behind the mobility and ubiquity of the chariot of God himself,[11] the character of Ezekiel's priesthood is transformed by his prophetic call: unlike his contemporaries who always serve the deity of a particular shrine, this priest serves a god whose "permanent residence" is paradoxically *mobile* and *ubiquitous;* consequently, he himself must be similarly mobile.

A god who is not tied to any city or shrine as a permanent abode but rather shows himself to be ubiquitous, is already no longer a local or national god but a universal one. And this is precisely how the Lord who commissions Ezekiel to speak on his behalf now appears. To be sure, the Lord who spoke through Amos, Isaiah, and Jeremiah did also address the nations as their de facto master; still, he was always first and foremost the deity of Jerusalem.[12] But now the priorities are suddenly reversed. In Ezekiel the Lord is the universal God who happens to be also the Lord of Jerusalem. His

9. Compare 2:3-7 with 3:4-11, and notice how the two passages are clearly linked by 2:8-3:3.
10. Notice the repetition of 2:2 in 3:24.
11. See 1:12, 20-21. Notice the prominence given to the notion of mobility through the statement that the spirit is "in the wheels" (vv.20 and 21). Also, the Hebrew *ruah* means simply "wind" or "breath"—i.e., not just air but *moving* air.
12. See Am 1:2; Is 1; 6; Jer 1.

primary abode is the mobile and ubiquitous chariot (ch.1), not Jerusalem. His glory, which Isaiah had contemplated in the temple (Is 6:1-4), and which Israel thought to be essentially linked to that location,[13] appears first to Ezekiel in Babylonia (1:1, 3; 3:15, 23). Moreover, Ezekiel reports that what resides in the temple's holy of holies is none other than God's chariot, specifically the chariot first seen in Babylonia (10:1-22, especially vv.15, 20, and 22). Thus, the temple and Jerusalem are no longer God's sole or even primary residence but rather just one of the places he visits.

A Radically New Reading of the Past

The new understanding of the Lord as universal God necessitated a re-reading of the basic traditions of Judah. Until Ezekiel, the point of departure for Judah's self-understanding, and consequently for Judah's understanding of its deity, was Jerusalem and the temple.[14] Jerusalem was the center of the Lord's world, the locus of all his activity. From his perspective (so thought Judah) not only were all the other nations relatively unimportant but even the northern kingdom of Israel—the original source of Judah's own belief in Yahweh![15]—was relegated to second rank as renegade nation or at best mere precursor of Judah.[16]

A complete turnabout occurred with Ezekiel. The relationship between the Lord and Jerusalem was no longer perceived as an eternal and immutable "marriage made in heaven." And the new idea of the Lord as the universal God who stands alone, neither dependent on nor defined by anything else such as a city or shrine, had as its necessary corollary the rejection of faith in Jerusalem as the divine city guaranteed permanent protection from earthly peril. Ezekiel even promised it punitive destruction:

13. See Ex 40:34-35; 1 Kg 8:10-12.
14. See vol.1, pp.12-13, 47-48, 59-66.
15. See vol.1, pp.23-31, 51.
16. See 1 Kg 12-13; Ps 78, especially vv.67-68.

Again the word of the Lord came to me: "Son of man, make known to Jerusalem her abominations, and say, Thus says the Lord God to Jerusalem:...on the day you were born your navel string was not cut, nor were you washed with water to cleanse you, nor rubbed with salt, nor swathed with bands. No eye pitied you...And when I passed by you, and saw you weltering in your blood, I said to you in your blood, 'Live and grow up like a plant of the field.' And you grew up and became tall and arrived at full maidenhood...yet you were naked and bare. When I passed by you again and looked upon you, behold you were at the age for love; and I spread my skirt over you, and covered your nakedness: yea, I plighted my troth to you and entered into a covenant with you, says the Lord God, and you became mine....I clothed you also with embroidered cloth and shod you with leather, I swathed you in fine linen and covered you with silk....And your renown went forth among the nations because of your beauty, for it was perfect through the splendor which I had bestowed upon you, says the Lord God. But you trusted in your beauty, and played the harlot because of your renown, and lavished your harlotries on any passer-by....Wherefore, O harlot, hear the word of the Lord: Thus says the Lord God, Because your shame was laid bare and your nakedness uncovered in your harlotries with your lovers, and because of all your idols, and because of the blood of your children that you gave to them, therefore, behold, I will gather all your lovers, with whom you took pleasure, all those you loved and all those you loathed; I will gather them against you from every side, and will uncover your nakedness to them...And I will give you into the hand of your lovers, and they shall throw down your vaulted chamber and break down your lofty places; they shall strip you of your clothes and take your fair jewels, and leave you naked and bare. They shall bring up a host against you, and they shall stone you and cut you to pieces with their swords....Because you have not remembered the days of your youth, but have enraged me with all these things; therefore, behold, I will requite your deeds upon your head, says the Lord God. (16:1-43)

Far from enjoying permanent, unconditional, special status and protection as the Lord's home, Jerusalem has now dropped so low as to be worse than rebellious Samaria, even worse than that epitome of sin and moral corruption, Sodom itself:

And your elder sister is Samaria, who lived with her daughters to the north of you; and your younger sister, who lived to the south of you, is Sodom with her daughters. Yet you were not content to walk in their ways, or do according to their abominations; within a very little time you were more corrupt than they in all your ways....you have committed more abominations than they, and have made your sisters appear righteous by all the abominations which you have committed....because of your sins in which you acted more abominably than they, they are more in the right than you. So be ashamed, you also, and bear your disgrace, for you have made your sisters appear righteous. (16:46-52)

A New (Kind of) Exodus

The re-interpretation of the past finds its highest expression in ch.20, where we encounter a new outlook on the exodus, the original, definitive epiphany of the Lord to his people.[17] Not only is the subsequent wilderness experience presented negatively as one of continued and stubborn sinfulness and apostasy (vv.13-26), but even while still in Egypt the people were rebellious—so much so that God delivered them from Egypt not to save them but only to keep them from sullying his reputation since he was known as their God! (vv.7-10, 14, 22) This notion of rebelliousness beginning already in Egypt is new and is introduced here because it is at the heart of Ezekiel's concept of the new exodus: the prophet's intention is to point out the similarity in situation as well as attitude between the Judahites in Babylonia and their forefathers in Egypt.[18]

However, that does not mean the new exodus can be taken for granted because God will have to act again for his name's sake regardless of the evils of his people. The "elders of Israel" made just that mistake: they assumed the Lord had no choice in the matter, the only uncertainty being his timetable (v.1). Their complacency had to be rebuked, and that explains God's refusal to be inquired of by them as well as his condemnation of them (vv.3-4).

Yes, says Ezekiel, the Lord acted for his name's sake in the original exodus; but there was nothing automatic about it. It was always the Lord, the divine person constrained by no one, who acted of his own

17. See vol.1, pp.39-48.
18. Compare vv.30-31 with v.8.

free will. It was his decision, his action, and exclusively for *his name's sake*; and in spite of whatever the elders may think, he will not be caught at his own game. This time, and in the sight of all nations, he will lead the Judahites out of Babylonia and into the wilderness, and the nations will see with their own eyes that he is almighty. But afterward he will settle the score with his people, as soon as they are out of sight of the nations. This time, the Lord's ultimate intention behind his mighty deed will be not so much to "save" the Judahites as to "be king over" them (v.33), i.e., to use his punishing rod (v.37)[19] in order to judge them (v.36b) and purge out the rebel transgressors from among them (v.38). Furthermore, at this juncture he reveals that this had been his intention even when he "saved" their fathers from Egypt long ago (v.36a). What was all along wrongly perceived by them as weakness on his part or a convenient way for them to get what they wanted out of him without any reciprocal responsibilities, was merely his mercy through which he was teaching them time and again to recognize him, and only him, as their true, beneficent king (vv.39-45).

A New (Kind of) Israel

The people of God will survive the purging process undiminished: "*all* the house of Israel, *all* of them" (20:40) will serve the Lord as their king afterwards. The reason Israel in its entirety must survive and continue to serve the Lord is once again to preserve his holy name from profanation by the nations (20:39, 41). Ezekiel's repeated emphasis on the importance of preserving the Lord's reputation among foreign peoples[20] reflects his understanding of God's universality. His point is that the issue of the Lord's status as God[21] is not a private matter between him and Israel but rather a public matter between him and all humanity.

19. On the rod's use in punishment, see Is 11:4.

20. See also Ezek 39:21-29.

21. "I will manifest my holiness" means essentially, "I will show myself to be God." See comments on Am 4:2.

And since the nations see the Lord as Israel's God as much as Judah's, he must take action to protect and preserve both in order to preserve his image untarnished in their eyes.

This perspective on the Lord's relationship to his people and the reasons for his behavior toward them is fundamental to Ezekiel's message. It can be clearly seen in the following key text linking Ezekiel's message about the judgment of Jerusalem and the "new exodus" (chs.1-39) with his prophecy of the future "new Jerusalem" (chs.40-48):

> And I will set my glory among the nations; and all the nations shall see my judgment which I have executed, and my hand which I have laid on them. The house of Israel shall know that I am the Lord their God, from that day forward. And the nations shall know that the house of Israel went into captivity for their iniquity, because they dealt so treacherously with me that I hid my face from them and gave them into the hand of their adversaries, and they all fell by the sword. I dealt with them according to their uncleanness and their transgressions, and hid my face from them.
>
> Therefore thus says the Lord God: Now I will restore the fortunes of Jacob, and have mercy upon the whole house of Israel; and I will be jealous for my holy name. They shall forget their shame, and all the treachery they have practiced against me, when they dwell securely in their land with none to make them afraid, when I have brought them back from the peoples and gathered them from their enemies' lands, and through them have vindicated my holiness in the sight of many nations. Then they shall know that I am the Lord their God because I sent them into exile among the nations, and then gathered them into their own land. I will leave none of them remaining among the nations any more; and I will not hide my face any more from them, when I pour out my spirit upon the house of Israel, says the Lord. (39:21-29)[22]

We see here a belief in oneness and completeness as essential characteristics of God's Israel, a tenet destined to become a hall-

22. This passage is closely related to the one in ch.20 discussed above. See the parallels between: 21a and 20:41b; 22a and 20:42a; 23c ("they all") and 20:40 ("all of them"); 25b and 20:40a (the Hebrew behind "the whole house of Israel" and "all the house of Israel" is identical); 25c and 20:9, 14, 22, 39, 44; 27a and 20:41a; 27b and 20:41b; 28a and 20:42a.

mark of Judaism. The idea that God's people must be a single, undivided entity, one which would necessarily include both Israel and Judah, began with Jeremiah and Ezekiel. It is apparent in the way they frequently bring the northern kingdom into the picture when discussing the demise of Judah or its eventual restoration.[23] The last such instance in Ezekiel (37:15-28) immediately follows the famous "dry bones" passage (37:1-14), and together these texts provide clear evidence of Ezekiel's redefinition of the term "house of Israel." In vv.1-14 we hear that: (a) the dry bones are "the whole house of Israel"; (b) this Israel as a whole is dead; and (c) its resurrection will happen in the same valley/plain (vv.1-2) mentioned in 3:22-23, at the same spot where the original encounter between God, Ezekiel, and the *Judahite* exiles (3:14-15) took place.[24] The impression this leaves regarding Ezekiel's expansion of the term "Israel" to include the people originally belonging to the southern kingdom as well as to the northern one is confirmed in the following passage, which calls the people of Judah "the children of Israel" (v.16a), the people of Ephraim (i.e., Israel proper) "the house of Israel" (v.16b), and their union "the children of Israel" (v.21).[25]

All this indicates that Ezekiel has redefined the nature of God's people. His understanding may be termed a *new (kind of) Israel*,[26] and it entails a reinterpretation of the previously separate histories of

---

23. See Jer 3:6-18; 7:1-15; 23:1-8; 31:27-28; 33:14-26; Ezek 16:45-58; 23:1-49; 37:15-28. Conversely, passages originally about Ephraim were edited to include Judah; see comments above on Jer 30-31.

24. The identity of the location can be gathered from the following: (a) the same Hebrew word *biq'ah* is used in both places (RSV has "plain," with "valley" in a footnote, at 3:22-23; and "valley," with "plain" in a footnote, at 37:1-2); (b) in Ezekiel *biq'ah* occurs only at 3:22-23 and 37:1-2, and at 8:4 in reference to 3:22-23; (c) the expression "the hand of the Lord was upon me" is found only at 3:22 and 37:1 in Ezekiel; and (d) in both places that expression is combined with a form of the verb *yasa'* (go forth; bring out in *hiphil*), a combination found nowhere else in Ezekiel.

25. RSV translates "people of Israel," but the Hebrew is the same as in v.16a.

26. See also my comments on "the Israel of God" in Gal 6:16 in my *Galatians: A Commentary*, SVS Press (Crestwood: 1994).

Judah and Israel into one history of this new Israel.[27] Moreover, this new Israel is defined solely from the eschatological perspective of God's ultimate intervention in human affairs to bring it into being: already it is considered the only true Israel even though it does not even exist yet.[28] It is this view that influenced nascent Judaism in its editing of all previous material pertaining to the origins of Israel (the Pentateuch),[29] the history of the two kingdoms (the Deuteronomistic History), the prophetic literature,[30] and the literature it produced itself (Chronicles and Ezra-Nehemiah)—in other words, all of what eventually came to be known as the scripture of Judaism.

A New (Kind of) Order

The new (kind of) exodus that produced a new (kind of) Israel was to be sealed with a new (kind of) covenant that would be (unlike the old one) truly eternal.[31] In order to effect this, a new (kind of) order was needed, one radically different from the previous order, one that would not allow, even as a remote possibility, a breach in the relationship between God and his people. According to Ezekiel's predecessors—Amos, Hosea, Micah, Isaiah, Zephaniah, and Jeremiah—the ill was an integral part of the "old" order itself, which is but the typical order of socio-political life: a city-state or kingdom, in the midst of which rules a king who acts as the deity's plenipotentiary representative yet is never able to properly fulfill this duty. That is to say, for all practical purposes, the ill lay in the institution of kingship.[32]

27. Such shifts in perspective or reinterpretations are common in historiography; see the discussion in vol.1, pp.17-21.
28. Notice the absolute identity between the dead (old, present) Israel and the raised (new, eschatological) one in 37:11-14.
29. See vol.1, pp.126-145.
30. See comments above on Am 9:9-15 and Hos 1-3.
31. See 37:25-28; see also 43:7, 9.
32. This prophetic criticism of kingship found its culmination in Deuteronomy (see 17:14-20) and the Deuteronomistic History (see 1 Sam 8:10-18).

Ezekiel agrees:

1) He singles out the institution itself as the target of harsh invective during the last days of Jerusalem in 587. Ch.34 is a direct attack against *all* past kings of Judah and Israel.

2) In the new order it is God himself who will rule directly, without the intermediacy of a king, over his people. The new David is intentionally called "prince" rather than king,[33] as are all rulers of the new Jerusalem.[34]

The direct rule of God is reflected in the utopian setup of the new order: the new socio-political entity revolves around the temple. The natural order of human society begins with the people themselves and the land they live on, and from that develop city, palace, and temple; but here it is the temple which defines the whole of the new reality (Ezek 40-48). In other words, this new order is utterly divine; and no wonder, since everything—God himself, his temple/city abode, his prophet/priest Ezekiel, and *all* Israel—is infused with his spirit. Jerusalem, the new abode of God as well as of Israel, is itself fully divine; its name is *yahweh šam* (the Lord is there; 48:35).

God's effectual kingship and the permanence of the new order are underscored by the prophecy about the battle with Gog, king of Magog (38:1-39:20), a mythical and eschatological passage which serves two related functions:

1) Upon his entrance into the new Jerusalem (43:1-12) God is declared to be king forever in the new Jerusalem, i.e., a king whose throne shall not be shaken by any eventual enemy.[35] With-

---

33. 34:24; 37:25. The use of *melek* (king) in reference to the new David in 37:22 is to be explained as corresponding to its parallel *mamlakot* (kingdoms) in the same verse: "...and *one king* shall be king over them; and they shall be no longer...divided into *two kingdoms.*" The same use of "king" to speak of David is repeated in v.24.

34. See 44:3; 45:7-9, 16-17, 22; 46:2, 4, 8, 10, 12, 16-18; 48:21-22. The kings, together with the rest of the people, are even prohibited from entering God's temple lest it be defiled (43:7-9).

35. The intimate connection between the notion of kingly rule and that of victory over enemies can be seen in the so-called messianic psalms praising God's anointed king at the occasion of his enthronement (Ps 2, 45, 72, 110).

out 38:1-39:20 there would have been no background for that proclamation.

2) The irrevocable, eternal establishment of the new Israel (37:1-14, 26-28) is tested and proven through its victory over the ultimate enemy, Gog of Magog and his hosts.[36]

The Influence of Ezekiel

Ezekiel's vision left a lasting stamp on nascent Judaism, detectable in both the content and form of its scriptures, especially the first part, the *torah*, or Pentateuch.[37] Genesis starts with the one and only universal God who creates the world and everything in it (chs.1-3) and is the god of all humanity and all nations (chs.2-11). It is this universal God who appears to Israel's forefather, Abraham, in Babylonia and leads him into an exodus toward Canaan (ch.12).

The same scenario applies later to the people of Israel: God's theophany takes place in the wilderness in conjunction with an exodus (Ex 19). What is remarkable here is that the entire instruction (*torah*) of God (Exodus, Leviticus, Numbers) is presented as originally taking place in the wilderness before the entry into Canaan and long before the rise of Jerusalem—and this despite the fact that its content revolves around the sanctuary and its service (Ex 24 through Num 10). Thus, the Pentateuchal *torah* that is supposed to guide every aspect of the life of Israel in Canaan and Jerusalem, is actually the *torah* of the one universal God who is not bound by any city or temple but rather who exists just as well in the wilderness, independent of any established institution or sanctuary.

Even Deuteronomy has been structured so as to conform to this line of thought. Despite its intended emphasis on Jerusalem it does not allow the Lord to become a prisoner of his city, because

36. This, by the way, confirms what I said earlier regarding the eschatological nature of the new (kind of) Israel.

37. See vol.1, pp.143-5.

here too the Lord constantly reminds his people that he did not first manifest himself from Jerusalem but from the wilderness. He fully and completely originated as God from the wilderness where there can be no life or being, except from the One who can generate life and being out of nothing. From beginning to end, the universal God of Genesis ch.1 is in fact the God of the entire Pentateuch, the text which contains the *entire* divine *torah*, the scripture par excellence of nascent Judaism.

The second scripture of nascent Judaism is termed "the prophets" and is comprised of "the prior prophets" (the six books constituting the Deuteronomistic History)[38] and "the latter prophets" (the books actually called by the names of prophets). The books of the prior prophets tell us how, after a good start under Joshua,[39] Israel in Canaan did not abide by the *torah* and thus ended up in the catastrophe of annihilation, i.e., exile into Babylonia, the land where its forefather Abraham had come from. The latter prophets tell us the reason behind Israel's demise and declare the new beginning God will bring out of it. Ezekiel's influence here is obvious in that the final editors of the collection deliberately arranged the material in each of the books bearing names of pre-exilic prophets to reflect the structure of the book of Ezekiel: beginning with prophecies of doom, they all end with the eschatological promise of the new Jerusalem.[40] This is also the overall structure of the second portion of scripture as a whole, since it ends with the eschatological oracles concerning the Lord's Day and the new Jerusalem (Zech 9:1-Mal 4:5).[41]

38. Joshua, Judges, 1 and 2 Samuel, and 1 and 2 Kings.
39. Note how closely the present book of Joshua corresponds to Ez 38-48: the procession into the land of the victorious Lord (chs.3-6 vs. Ez 38-43) followed by the partition of the land (chs.13-21 vs. Ez 47:13-48:29).
40. See Amos, Hosea, Micah, Isaiah, Obadiah, Zephaniah. See also Habakkuk with its final chapter on God's epiphany, battle, and triumph; and Nahum with its oracle of doom against Nineveh cast as a message of hope to Judah (1:9-10, 12-13; 2:1).
41. See comments below on those oracles. Notice also how the first part, the prior prophets, also ends on a positive note (2 Kg 25:27-30).

12

Second Isaiah

With the rise of the Persian empire under Cyrus I in the mid-6th century B.C., the days of Neo-Babylonian hegemony in the Near East were numbered. Yet it was not only the Persian conquerors who had occasion to be pleased with the turn of events that finally led to the fall of Babylon in 539/538. Many of the Babylonians themselves were eagerly anticipating an end to the reign of their despotic king, Nabonidus; and exiled subject peoples had not only that to rejoice about but also the prospect of being allowed to return to their land and exercise self-government.[1] Thanks to his policy of tolerance for local cultures, Cyrus' advance was widely greeted with euphoric optimism, an attitude plainly shared by a Judahite exile reared in the "school of Isaiah"[2] who left us the oracles found in chs.40-55 of Isaiah. He is referred to among scholars as Second Isaiah or Deutero-Isaiah, and his prophecies are often called the "Book of the Consolation of Israel."

Characteristics of Second Isaiah's Message

1) Second Isaiah is the first among the canonical prophets whose message consists entirely of good news. This is reflected in the opening declaration "Comfort, comfort my people, says the Lord" (40:1) as well as in the high incidence of both the verb *niham* (to comfort/console)[3] and the participle *m^ebasser* (messenger of good news)[4] from the verb *bisser* (to bear good news).

1. See vol.1, p.143.
2. See introductory comments on the book of Isaiah.
3. 40:1 (twice); 49:13; 51:3 (twice); 51:12; 51:19; 52:9.
4. 40:9 (twice); 41:27; 52:7 (twice). Usually translated "herald of good tidings" in RSV.

2) Jerusalem occupies a position of prominence,[5] due to the special interest given it by the school of Isaiah as well as by Ezekiel.[6]

3) Jeremiah and Ezekiel were the first to proclaim the Lord as the one, universal God, but Second Isaiah carried that idea to its logical conclusion: the Lord is the creator of the world and master of its destiny, and there are no other gods besides him. All other supposed deities are mere idols, inanimate objects no more powerful than the wood or stone they were fashioned from.[7]

4) God's salvation is specifically viewed as redemption.[8] In human terms, the "redeemer" in ancient Hebrew society was generally the closest kin of a man who had been forced to sell his property, or himself into slavery, to pay a debt: the redeemer's duty was to buy back the sold property or purchase the man's freedom, in order to preserve the family and its property intact.[9] The rules were quite rigid, requiring that if a more distant relative wished to act as the redeemer he would have to have the permission of the rightful go'el. Conversely, it was considered shameful for the closest relative to refuse to fulfill what was not only a right but a duty. Thus, in proclaiming himself as Israel's go'el (50:1-2a) the Lord was reminding both Israel and the nations that he had not forfeited his right. Despite what either group might be inclined to think, God was determined to exercise his right to keep Israel within his own sphere of influence and not allow it to be alien-

5. See Is 40:1-11; 44:24-28; 48:1-2; 51:17-23; 52:1-3, 7-10. See also 54:11-17 where the mention of stones, foundations, pinnacles, gates, and wall (vv.11-12) clearly refer to a city, presumably Jerusalem.
6. See comments on Ezek chs.40-48.
7. See 40:12-31; 41:22-29; 44:9-20, 24-28; 45:9-25. Even the Gentile king Cyrus was raised up by the Lord to do his bidding; see comments below on the first "servant" poem.
8. Notice the high incidence of the verb ga'al (to redeem; 43:1; 44:22, 23; 48:20; 52:3) and the participial noun go'el (redeemer; 41:14; 43:14; 44:6, 24; 47:4; 48:17; 49:7, 26; 54:5, 8).
9. See Lev 25:25-33, 48-55; see also 27:16-33. The go'el also bore a responsibility to father children for a man who had died without an heir, again in order to preserve the family (Deut 25:5-10; Gen 38), and if the man had been murdered, the go'el haddam (redeemer of blood) would avenge the crime (Num 35:19-27). The best example of the rules of redemption in actual practice is in Ruth (3:9, 12; 4:1-15).

ated, either by others or itself. Essentially, Second Isaiah is rendering in positive terms what Ezekiel before him had expressed negatively as invective against Israel: both prophets stress God's unimpeachable rule over Israel, his prerogative to "make woe or make weal" (Is 45:7) as he sees fit. In other words, Israel may refuse to accept God's salvation, but it cannot decide not to let him save! He will not allow Israel to make him appear to others as if he were in fact not a *go'el,* a redeeming/saving God.[10]

5) No less important than God's work of salvation as redemption is his original work of creation; in fact, the two are ultimately inseparable.[11] Although it may seem strange to our modern Western mentality shaped by ancient Greek as well as European medieval philosophy, creation was perceived dynamically in the ancient Near East, not statically as a one-shot deal. The created realm could not exist ipso facto, through its own innate power of being; it had to be constantly sustained by its creator. To keep his creation from ceasing to be, the power of the creating deity was required to continually preserve it from adverse and destructive powers represented by either the chaotic waters or the lifeless desert, both of which were perceived as domains of nothingness and death.[12] In Second Isaiah's eyes the Lord is creator in the same absolute and uncompromising way as he is savior, and Israel is his handicraft on either count.

6) If Israel was brought into being by the Lord and must be constantly kept alive by the Lord, then its relationship to him can only be that of servant to master. Hence the notion of Israel as the Lord's *'ebed* (servant/slave).[13]

7) The section of the book of Isaiah ascribed to Second Isaiah contains four poems or songs dealing with an unnamed "servant of the Lord" who is entrusted with a mission to Israel (42:1-4; 49:1-6; 50:4-9; 52:13-53:12). The difficulty inherent in these texts

10. See 42:18-25; 48:1-11, 16-19.
11. See 45:11-13, 15-18, 21-24; 51:9-16.
12. See 43:16-21; 44:2-5; 44:24-28.
13. 41:8-9; 42:19; 44:1-2, 21, 26; 45:4; 48:20.

is reflected in the fact that over the centuries scholars have proposed the widest possible range of answers to the obvious question regarding the identity of the "servant" but are no closer to a consensus now than when they started. The proposed interpretations can be divided into two main groups: individual versus collective.[14] In favor of the former, suffice it to say that the terminology used in all four poems taken in its most direct sense suggests an individual.[15] Actually, had it not been for the express identification of the servant as Israel in 49:3[16] and the frequent reference to Israel as the Lord's servant in Second Isaiah, it would not have even crossed anyone's mind that the servant in the four poems could be anything but an individual. Therefore it is safer to study these texts first having in mind an individual, and, only in case of compelling reasons to do so, probe the other possibility afterwards. The remainder of this section on Second Isaiah will be devoted to just such a study.

The First Poem (Is 42:1-4)

This text introduces a person chosen by God to carry out a specific mission. What is unique here is not that God upholds him, or chooses him, or delights in him, or puts his Spirit upon him, nor even that his mission is to administer justice. These are also characteristics of one or more different kinds of divinely appointed persons, such as king, priest, and prophet. What is particular to this servant is that his *mišpat* (justice/[just] judgment) he will bring forth not just to Israel but *to the nations*.

The centrality of this thought in the author's mind can be gathered from its repetition in vv.3c and 4bc,[17] and especially

14. E.g. Moses, David, Josiah, Isaiah, Jeremiah, Cyrus, Second Isaiah himself, the Messiah, and the eschatological prophet, on the one hand; and Israel, the new Israel, and the holy remnant, on the other.

15. See especially 42:1, 3c, 4; 49:1, 4-6; 50:4-7; 53:3, 7, 9-12.

16. This remark is not as compelling as it may seem; see comments on it below.

17. The word *torah* ([just] law/instruction) is parallel in meaning to *mišpat*.

from the fact that this sets up an *inclusio*[18] with v.1d. More specifically, the *inclusio* is formed by vv.1d and 3c, since the two lines are virtually identical in both wording and structure:

mišpat laggoyim yoseh (v.1d)
> (just) judgment to the nations he will bring forth

l'emet yoseh mišpat (v.3c)
> faithfully/truthfully[19] he will bring forth (just) judgment

These lines bracket a well-knit poetic passage written according to the rules of poetic parallelism[20] as well as inversion.[21] Not only is each of vv.2 and 3ab composed of two lines forming a synonymic parallel, but the entire section vv.1d-3 forms an inversion of the ABB'A' pattern: v.1d (A), v.2 (B), v.3ab (B'), v.3c (A'). The paradoxical message conveyed in this passage is that the servant will carry out his kingly role of implementing God's *mišpat* without using the corresponding royal instruments of power—the spoken word and the iron rod.[22] A stranger turn of events can hardly be imagined: the Lord's servant will implement the divine *mišpat* among the nations not by rewarding good and punishing evil but by remaining passive—by doing nothing!

This interpretation is corroborated by the wording of v.4 which informs us that he will not *yikheh* (fail/burn dimly) and he will not *yarus* (be discouraged/bruised), using the same verbs which in v.3 describe respectively the wick he will not quench (v.3b) and the reed he will not break (v.3a).[23] Thus, not only will the servant

18. An *inclusio* (Latin, meaning "inclusion") is a device according to the scheme A...A' whereby the main thought opens as well as concludes a passage, bracketing the entire passage. Its purpose is to clearly indicate to the hearer or reader the main thought or subject matter of the passage.

19. Literally, "to/unto faithfulness/truth." Notice the parallelism in Hebrew due to the use of the same preposition *l* (to) before "nations" in v.1d and "faithfulness/truth" in v.3c.

20. See comments on Am 2:6.

21. See comments on Am 5:4-5.

22. Compare this with the messianic prophecy in Is 11:3-4.

23. The intended parallelism is further underscored by the inversion pattern: *rasus* (bruised; passive participle of the verb *rasas;* v.3a), *kehah* (dimly burning; derived from the verb *kahah;* v.3b), *yikheh* (imperfect of *kahah;* v.4aa), *yarus* (imperfect of *rasas;* v.4ab). Even if *yarus* is the imperfect of *rus* (to flee/run away), the effect will still be the same.

be inactive, but his behavior seems to be connected with some kind of pressures or difficulties or persecutions he will have to suffer. In other words, *silence* and *suffering* are the paradoxical trade-marks of this divine messenger in the implementation of a "kingly" mission which would normally entail divine utterance and divine victory.[24] The paradox is all the more stunning when one takes into consideration that the basic mission of this servant is to bring forth God's *mišpat* to the nations to whom the Lord, in Second Isaiah, is intending to show that he is the one, universal God controlling the destinies of both Israel and the nations.

But what exactly does "*mišpat* among the nations" mean? A solid starting point for an investigation into the significance of this phrase would be v.4c, where the terms "earth" and "coast-lands" parallel "nations" in v.1d. "Earth" is too general a word to yield any help, but Second Isaiah's usage of *'iyyim* (coast-lands/islands) is more specific and its use relatively restricted, being confined to 40:15; 41:1, 5; 42:4, 10, 12, 15; 49:1; 51:5. From these and other Old Testament texts one can easily gather that *'iyyim* are stretches of land bordering on or surrounded by water[25] and thus are to be understood as islands or coastlands. In the mind of the ancient Israelite/Judahite such lands represent the far ends of the earth[26] or the (other) peoples/nations.[27] When *'iyyim* is not qualified by the name of a specific nation, it connotes *all* the nations, as far as the ends of the earth.

Now, returning to the occurrences of this word in Second Isaiah, we find that most of them appear in conjunction with *mišpat*:[28]

24. Compare with Cyrus who is granted victory over the nations when acting on behalf of the Lord (45:1-7).
25. See especially 42:10, 15; see also 11:11; 24:15; Esth 10:1.
26. See 41:5; 42:10; 49:1. See also 66:19; Ps 97:1; Jer 31:10.
27. See 40:15; 41:1; 42:11-12; 51:4-5. See also Gen 10:5; Jer 2:10; 47:4; Ezek 27:6-7; Zeph 2:11 ("lands" in RSV).
28. 5 out of 9 (or 5 out of 7 if one counts the pairs in 41:1 and 5, and in 42:10 and 12, as single instances each). Note that RSV translates *mišpat* variously in these texts as "judgment," or "justice," or "right."

40:14-15; 41:1; 42:4; 49:1-4; 51:4-5. For the purposes of our investigation we can dismiss the last three, since the third is the passage we are trying to clarify, while the fourth and fifth are too closely related to the servant texts to provide independent evidence.[29] That leaves the first two. These appear in passages where the Lord's universal glory is underscored in contradistinction to the vanity of the nations' deities and the powerlessness of their earthly leaders.[30] In the first, God is asserting his status as the one universal God by stating that he did not learn *mišpat* from anyone else, either humans or their supposed deities (40:15-26); in the second, he is ready to appear alongside the nations and their deities (41:21-29) in order to face *mišpat* (here obviously in the sense of judgment) together with them.

These texts lead to the conclusion that *mišpat* in Second Isaiah bears the connotation of a showdown between the Lord on the one hand, and the nations and their deities on the other. This showdown will vindicate him as the sole, universal God since it will reveal that Cyrus himself, the victorious king *of the nations,* was raised up by none other than the Lord himself (41:2-4; 45:1-13; 48:12-15). The same word *mišpat* at once designates both the process (the showdown) and its outcome (God's victory). As for the latter, the "justice" which arises from this "judgment" is more specifically to be understood as the Lord's own *torah,*[31] with which he had originally graced Israel and under which he is now intending to bring all the nations of the earth, so that both groups may enjoy his everlasting covenant (55:3-5).

29. While 51:4-5 is not itself part of a servant poem, its statement that "a *torah* will go forth from me, and my *mišpat* for a light to the nations" closely parallels the first and second ones (see 42:1d, 4c and 49:4b, 6b).

30. See 40:12-31 and 41:41:1-7, 21-29.

31. See especially 51:4 where the Lord says: "Listen to me, my people...for a *torah* will go forth from me, and my *mišpat* for a light to the peoples. My deliverance draws near speedily, my salvation has gone forth...the coastlands wait for me, and for my arm they hope." Notice the correspondence in terminology with 49:6 where the servant is entrusted with *one* mission to both Israel and the nations, its object being "that my salvation may reach to the end of the earth."

If the texts from which we inferred this unique dual meaning of *mišpat* were unrelated to the first servant poem, assigning the same meaning to its use there might be questionable. But such is not the case. A close look at 41:1 and 42:4 will reveal that they form an *inclusio*: in the former, the *'iyyim* are called for a *mišpat*, and in the latter, they await the Lord's *torah/mišpat*. Apparently the entire passage 41:1-42:4 is a single literary unit within which the first servant poem was intended to be read and understood. Other facts point to the same conclusion:

1) The *'iyyim* are addressed directly (second person rather than third person) only twice in Second Isaiah, in 41:1 and in 49:1. Since 49:1 is the beginning of the second servant poem where the servant himself is speaking, the virtually identical wording of 41:1 may well indicate that the speaker there is not the Lord but the servant, who is calling the *'iyyim* to appear with him for a show-down *(mišpat)*. Indeed, during the actual debate with the *'iyyim* God is referred to in the third person (41:21).

2) Following each of the first two poems is a passage that begins with "Thus says the Lord" and addresses the servant in a similar way, which betrays an intended parallelism between them.[32] In the second, the expression "Thus says the Lord" is warranted by the change of speaker from the servant (vv.1-6) to God (vv.7-12). In the case of the first poem, however, this change does not make sense unless one assumes that the divine words of vv.1-4 are part of a speech by the servant that started at 41:1, in the same way as the divine words of 49:6 are part of the servant speech in 49:1-6.

3) The word "behold" appears numerous times in 41:1-42:4 (41:11, 15, 24, 29, 42:1). Each of the ones prior to 42:1 introduces a statement by God in support of his claim to be the sole master of both Israel and the nations, so 42:1-4 may well have been intended as yet another such statement.

32. 42:5-9 and 49:7-12, respectively. Compare 42:6 with 49:8, and 42:7 with 49:9a.

The reading of 41:1-42:4 as one literary unit integrates the first servant poem into the entire message of Second Isaiah. Though endowed with a messianic commission (44:28-45:1), Cyrus is only a cover for God's real messenger, the servant. His rise to power and liberation of those subjugated by Babylon, including the Judahites, is just the occasion for the Lord's real message,[33] namely that he, and only he, is the master of the whole world's destiny: the liberator Cyrus as well as the liberated Israel and the liberated nations have only him as God. The total absence of David as an eschatological figure in Second Isaiah[34]—as well as Third Isaiah, for that matter—is intended to underscore God's direct kingship in the process of the post-exilic restoration. For Second Isaiah, unlike Ezekiel,[35] it is God *alone* who will be the eschatological ruler, with no intermediary. Chs.40-55 abound with passages describing the Lord's creating activity or referring to him as king or sole God.[36]

In order to reserve the unique role of eschatological ruler exclusively for himself, God assigns two essentially "kingly" functions to two different individuals, thereby splitting the unsplittable and leaving neither of them as a "king" in the sense that David would have been. The function of leading armies to victory over enemies, and the glory and power resulting from that, he gives to Cyrus; the administration of justice (*mišpat*) he allots to the servant.[37] Both together would be required for any individual to be considered king in the fullest sense, that of God's plenipotentiary representative.

However, the two functions are not of equal importance, the

33. See comments above on Jer 1 where I show that the siege of Jerusalem by the Babylonians was only the opportunity for God to show the real siege, that of Jeremiah and his God by Jerusalem.
34. David is mentioned only once as the historical past figure to whom the promises about to be fulfilled were made (55:3).
35. See Ezek 34:23-24; 37:24-25 and comments on them above.
36. 40:12-31; 41:21-29; 42:10-13; 43:8-12, 15-21; 44:6-20, 24-28; 45:9-13; 51:4-11; 52:7-12.
37. Some key texts which ascribe these functions to the king are: 1 Kg 3:16-28; Ps 45:4-7; 72:1-15; 97; 99:1-5; 110:5-6.

former being clearly subservient to the latter: according to 41:1 it is through *mišpat* (in the sense of "judgment") that God's victory will be settled, and then it will be through *mišpat* (in the sense of "justice") that God will rule and build up the world he has conquered.[38] Hence the superiority of the servant over Cyrus in God's plan: although the Lord will subjugate kings under Cyrus (41:2), "kings [including Cyrus?] shall shut their mouths because of him [the servant]; for that which has not been told them they shall see, and that which they have not heard they shall understand" (52:15). What they will be given to understand is precisely that the servant too will be granted divine victory (53:12a). It is then the servant who, in God's time, will be shown to be his plenipotentiary representative in that he will ultimately combine in himself both divine functions of victory and *mišpat*.

The Second Poem (Is 49:1-6)

Here too the basic theme is the servant's mission to the nations. At the start the servant addresses his declaration to the *'iyyim* and the "peoples from afar" (v.1a), and at the end God explains the ultimate purpose of his servant's mission by saying, "It is too light a thing that you should be my servant to raise up the tribes of Jacob and to restore the preserved of Israel; I will give you as a light to the nations, that my salvation may reach to the end of the earth." (v.6) As an indication of its relative importance, note that this statement quotes God directly, while the mission to Jacob/Israel described in v.5 is not a quotation at all but rather a relative clause identifying the Lord who speaks in v.6.

Still, the mention of the mission to Israel cannot be written off as an insignificant digression, since it does take up one fourth of the poem (vv.5-6a) and begins with the same "called from the

38. Notice how the servant's mission is the last in a series of texts introduced with "behold"; the others, which herald Cyrus' rise to power and victory, lead up to it as to a conclusion (see above).

womb" formula with which the servant introduces himself in v.1b. Besides, v.6 suggests the two missions are closely related, more like two aspects of one mission than two separate missions.[39]

Therefore, understanding the mission to Israel is vital to understanding the whole poem. As summarized in vv.5b-6a, the object of that mission is: "to bring Jacob back to the Lord...that Israel might be gathered to him...to raise up the tribes of Jacob and to restore the preserved of Israel." This language is unlike anything in the first servant poem, but consider the remarkable similarity between *mišpat/torah* and *yšu'ah/yeše'* (salvation/victory) as they appear in both of these poems and the closely related passage 51:4-5: God's *mišpat/torah* "goes forth/is brought forth" (42:1, 3; 51:4) as "a light to the peoples" (51:4), and the *'iyyim* "wait" for it; similarly, his *yeše'* "goes forth" (51:5) because the servant is "a light to the nations" (49:6), and the *'iyyim* "wait" for it (51:5). The servant who brings God's *mišpat/torah* "to the nations" in the first poem, is instrumental in making his salvation "reach to the end of the earth" in the second. Taking into consideration these similarities and the fact that the word *yšu'ah* also means "victory" (actually its original meaning),[40] we can conclude that the second poem's setting is the same as the first's, where the victory/salvation is Israel's in the sense that it is wrought by God *for* and *within* Israel (41:8-20). Accordingly, the servant's mission is meant to take place not only for Israel but within it.

That this mission to Israel is itself the content of the servant's mission to the nations, and not just a preamble to it, can be seen from the structure of the dialogue between the servant and God:

1) Each of vv.3-6 displays the same pattern: a statement about the servant's mission (or his call in the case of v.3) is followed by a

39. See also 51:4-5 which closely parallels the first two servant poems' phraseology regarding the mission to the nations, yet is explicitly addressed to Israel.

40. Compare also the verb *nikbad* (RSV: honored) and the noun *'oz* (RSV: strength) at the end of 49:5. The first means "to be glorified (by God)" and the second has the connotation of "(divine) power connected with victory."

statement about the positive result or realized purpose of that mission. Now, the mission to Israel is presented in the first part of v.5 and v.6, i.e., as part of the "mission statement" in those verses; but the mission to the nations finds expression only in the second part of v.6, i.e., in the "result/purpose statement."[41]

2) The mission to Israel in vv.5a and 6a parallels the servant's labor and spending of his strength in v.4a, suggesting that this is actually the part of his mission in which he takes action. But at the same time the notion in v.4a of effort expended in vain also recalls the paradoxical nature of the servant's mission and the idea there that he will carry it out under some kind of pressure, characteristics of the mission to the nations in the first poem.

3) The statement concerning the futility of the servant's work in v.4a parallels the term "servant" in v.3a, clearly indicating that the former reflects the essence of what it means to be the Lord's servant.[42] This finds confirmation in the emphatic "And now" at the beginning of v.5: *now* that the servant has fulfilled the conditions of his mission (v.4), as stipulated by the One who chose him (v.5), he is made privy to the ultimate scope of that mission (v.6).[43]

4) In that case, v.6 is not really commissioning the servant to a new mission. How could it, since his fate as God's servant was decided long ago, even from his mother's womb (v.3b, 5a)? Consequently, even v.3a is to be read not so much as a commissioning, but rather as a simple statement of fact, just as it sounds: "You are my servant." This reading of the text is corroborated by the servant's reaction, in which he confirms that statement by recall-

---

41. This is clear in the Hebrew original, but the nature of this *Introduction* does not allow a detailed discussion of the matter here.

42. If, as seems probable, 49:1-6 is structured according to poetic inversion, this would provide more evidence for the parallel between vv.3 and 4: A/the nations (v.1a); B/the call from the womb (vv.1b-2); C/the person of the servant (v.3); C'/the mission of the servant (v.4); B'/the call from the womb and mission to Israel (v.5); A'/the mission to the nations (v.6).

43. The "And now" ultimately introduces the statement in v.6 since all of v.5 is a relative clause qualifying the speaker.

ing what he has done in the past and expressing his expectation for the future: "I *have labored* in vain, I *have spent* my strength for nothing and vanity; *yet surely* my right is with the Lord, and my recompense with my God." (v.4) As he pronounces these words, the servant is positioned, as it were, between vv.4a and 4b, not at the beginning of v.4. That is to say, his work as a servant is already behind him,[44] and he is expressing his confidence[45] that the Lord who made him what he is, will surely bring about what he has in mind. It is only after the servant has performed his allotted task, and has reached the point of waiting patiently for God to bring fruition to his apparently fruitless work, that God reveals his ultimate intention (v.6).

Excursus: "Israel" in Is 49:3

Considering the servant's mission to Israel and his highly individual features,[46] it is hard to imagine that the term "Israel" in v.3 is not a scribal addition reflecting the first tendency toward a collective interpretation of the servant. We can see the same sort of thing in the Septuagint, which inserts "Jacob" before "my servant" and "Israel" after "my chosen" in 42:1.[47] But how is one to explain the inherent contradiction of naming the servant "Israel" in a passage where it is specifically stated that he has a mission to Israel? I believe this gloss was intended to preempt any possibility for the reader to identify the servant as being Cyrus. Needless to say, such

44. Whatever may still lie ahead for him to do—if anything—would only be to carry on what he has already been doing.

45. Notice the emphatic *'aken* (nevertheless; yet surely).

46. Such as his being "called from the womb" and "named from his mother's body" (v.1b).

47. These may well reflect the connection of the first servant poem with the preceding ch.41 in the glossator's mind. Notice how they conform to what we find in 45:4 ("my servant Jacob and Israel my chosen") where Cyrus is proclaimed as the liberator of Israel; this parallel would be inexplicable unless one admits the glossator made the connection between 42:1-4 and 41:1-5, where Cyrus is also called God's chosen one for the liberation of Israel. If so, then this is yet another indication that 41:1-42:4 is to be considered a literary unit (see above).

an interpretation would not have been palatable to a nascent Judaism that was growing to be more and more ethnically exclusive[48] and which was expecting the establishment of God's rule through the intermediacy of a (necessarily) Jewish Messiah whose mission would entail the liberation of Israel from all foreign powers.[49]

Without the gloss it would have been quite possible for someone to assume that Cyrus might be the servant of these four poems, especially of the second one, since it specifically mentions the raising up of Jacob and the restoration of Israel. Elsewhere Second Isaiah unequivocally calls Cyrus the Lord's shepherd (44:28) and anointed (i.e., messiah; 45:1), and consistently presents him as the liberator purposely raised up by God to bring salvation to Israel, the Lord's servant.[50] It is true that Cyrus is not once explicitly termed "servant," while Jacob/Israel is granted that appelative no less than nine times,[51] but the similarities between Cyrus and the protagonist of the four poems would nevertheless have made him a prime candidate for anyone attempting to identify the unnamed servant of the Lord. And those who wanted messianic prophecies to point to a Jewish Messiah would naturally have sought a way to prevent that.

The Third Servant Poem (Is 50:4-9)

This whole passage looks like an expansion of 49:4: vv.4-6 correspond to 49:4a (both describe the servant's difficult mission), and vv.7-9 parallel 49:4b (both express the servant's confidence in the Lord). By elaborating on already familiar themes it fills in some of the gaps in our knowledge about the servant.

48. See vol.1, pp.145-6.
49. If my thesis is correct, then it will confirm that the servant poems were viewed in at least some Jewish circles as being "messianic" already before the 1st century A.D.
50. See 41:2-3 in conjunction with vv.8-20; 44:28-45:4; 48:12-15; and 48:20 in conjunction with the second servant poem, which immediately follows it. Note also that 41:8-9, according to my reading, is to be read along with the first servant poem.
51. 41:8, 9; 42:19; 44:1, 2, 21, 26; 45:4; 48:20.

Here he introduces himself as a *limmud* (disciple; literally, one who is taught) of the Lord. As such, his business is not merely to learn (v.4c) but also to teach others what he is himself taught (v.4ab). In other words, he is assigned (as in 42:4c) the task of propagating the divine instruction or *torah*,[52] a duty typically belonging to king or priest. However, the servant's role is unlike those two in that he is more disciple than teacher: he is taught this *torah*, i.e., God's will, *every morning*. Whereas the others would look to a traditional *torah* established in the past and remaining as immutable as the written word used to preserve it, the servant is to *await* God's will in order to be able to dispense it, much as one would await a human king's commands each day. This feature would make of the servant a prophet in the likeness of Amos, Hosea, Isaiah, Jeremiah, and Ezekiel.[53] He even sounds like the ideal prophet, since he does not rebel against anything the Lord tells him and does not turn back from whatever task the Lord assigns him (v.5).

V.6 details the results of the servant's obedience, and by extension the content of the divine commandment to him. If he willingly suffers the indignities described here, it can only be because God's word decreed it. In other words, in the case of the servant, the word of prophecy not only "takes flesh" in the sense that it is fulfilled—as it did with the aforementioned prophets— but also in the more direct sense that it is borne by and expressed in the servant's own flesh. The third poem thus clarifies the ambiguous, if not cryptic, content of verses 42:4a and 49:4a in the

52. The close connection between the verb *lamad* (to learn) or its cognate *limmed* (to teach) on the one hand, and the *torah* with its commandments, statutes, testimonies, and judgments/ordinances on the other, can be seen from the usual occurrence of the former in conjunction with the latter in Deuteronomy, the book of the *torah* (4:1, 5, 10 [twice], 14; 5:1, 31; 6:1; 11:19, 17:19; 31:12, 13; i.e., 12 out of the 17 instances of *lamad* or *limmed*) and in Ps 119, the hymn to the *torah* and God's word (vv.7, 12, 26, 64, 66, 68, 71, 73, 108, 124, 135, 171; i.e., all instances of *lamad* or *limmed*).

53. On this difference between the prophetic word and the fixed *torah*, see the Introduction.

first two: it is the very person of the servant, or, more accurately, this person "put to shame," that expresses God's *torah/mišpat*.[54]

However, God's instructions to the servant must go beyond merely directing him to endure ill use: an integral part of the servant's obedient response is his complete confidence—while being put to shame by others—that God will indeed vindicate him ultimately (v.7).[55] Furthermore, this confidence is rooted in the fact that it is God who willed that he be put to shame, and the Lord will certainly vindicate and declare innocent the one who merely accepted and carried out his will (v.8-9). In summary, then, the content of God's eschatological *torah/mišpat* announced in the first three servant poems is essentially the servant dishonored, yet vindicated by God even in the midst of his dishonor.

But what about the specifics of the servant's experience: do the poems tell us where it takes place or who dishonors him? In fact, they do offer some indications. As we have seen, the servant experiences what he does as a direct result of his obedience to God's command (vv.5-6). Yet this can hardly be unrelated to the immediately preceding description of his mission as one of teaching (v.4). And where would he teach but among his peers, i.e., within Israel? This surmise is supported by the following facts:

1) The preamble to the third poem (50:1-3) is an indictment of Israel for its sins leading up to the exile (v.1b) and specifically reminds Israel that the Lord remains its *go'el* (v.2a).[56]

2) The third poem is followed by an appeal to follow the servant's example of confidence in the Lord despite difficulties in v.10 and a

54. Notice the use of *mišpat* in v.8. The RSV translates *ba'al mišpati* (literally, the master of my judgment; i.e., the one who stands against me during the process of my judgment) into "my adversary."

55. Notice how the servant's confidence in the Lord's (future) help (v.7a) is expressed as a present reality ("I have not been confounded" and "I have set my face like a flint" in v.7bc) *while* he is being put to shame (vv.5bc-6). Though sometimes translated differently in English versions, the Hebrew verbs in both cases are all in the same past tense (perfect form in Hebrew).

56. See above on the notion of *go'el*.

word of judgment against those who create those difficulties in v.11, which jibes well with his mission as a teacher/prophet.

3) The immediately following passage 51:1-8 sounds much like the second servant poem (especially vv.4-5) and calls upon Israel to "listen" (vv.1, 4a, 7)[57] and "give ear" (v.4a)[58] to the Lord. These verses' similarity to the servant's commission in 50:4-5 can hardly be happenstance; through this passage God may be asking Israel to hearken to the message he is sending it through and in his servant.

4) As discussed above, the second poem points to a mission which is to take place within Israel.

5) Throughout Second Isaiah, and interspersed among the servant poems, repeated allusions are made to Israel as a servant of the Lord[59] who is time and again sinning against him[60] by being blind and deaf to him.[61] Actually, God wanted to make his *torah* known through his servant Israel (42:21), but Israel refused to obey it (v.24). Finally, it is the Lord's servant Israel that the servant of the poems is trying to bring back to the Lord (49:5) and whose tribes he is to raise up and restore (49:6).

The Fourth Servant Poem (52:13-53:12)

The final poem in the series both recapitulates the contents of its predecessors and goes beyond them by offering a new interpretation of the servant's suffering and shame. The new idea can be found at the center of this long passage's chiastic structure:[62]

57. Also translated "hearken." In vv.1 and 7, it is the same verb *šamaʿ* found also at the end of 49:4.
58. *he'ezin,* the *hiphil* form of *'azan* from the noun *'ozen* (ear), used at the end of 50:4 and the beginning of 50:5.
59. 41:8, 9; 42:19; 44:1, 2, 21, 26, 45:4, 48:20.
60. 42:18-25; 43:22-28; 50:1-3.
61. 42:18, 19, 20, 23; see also 43:8; 48:8.
62. Chiasm is a literary device resembling an inversion with a center, according to the pattern ABCB'A' or ABCDC'B'A'. The central element has no correspondent and functions as the central point of the entire structure. (For an explanation of inversion, see comments on Am 5:4-5.)

A/52:13-15: the servant is glorified before kings;

B/53:1-3: the servant suffers and is humiliated;

C/vv.4-6: the servant's suffering is *for the sin of his fellows*;[63]

B'/vv.7-9: the servant's humiliation and suffering are unto death;

A'/vv.10-12: the servant is glorified before the great and the strong.[64]

Thus, the focus of the fourth servant poem is to be found in section C. Its theme was not even hinted at by the previous poems: the sins of the disobedient servant of the Lord, Israel, are to be expiated by the sufferings of this obedient servant of the Lord. The servant, then, holds the key to the restoration of Israel—which means it will not happen as a result of Israel's own spontaneous repentance and return to God. On the contrary, it appears rather that it will come about despite Israel's persistent disobedience. It is precisely this highly irregular *mišpat* of the Lord that is the stunning news to be carried to the nations, who, in their turn, acknowledge it as indeed *mišpat*.

Yet these verses, important as they are, reflect only part of the story. Recognition of the poem's chiastic structure should not obscure the fact that, like any poem, it is meant to be read from beginning to end. Such a progressive reading will lead to a fuller understanding of the servant's role. The opening verse 52:13 already predicts the servant's eventual triumphal exaltation in no uncertain terms: he will be "exalted" and "lifted up" as high as the divine King himself.[65] Before that, however, he must endure some kind of abasement which will reduce him to virtually "subhuman" status. Meanwhile, as this story unfolds, the whole course of his

63. This section's character as a turning point in the poem is announced by the emphatic *'aken* (yet surely) in v.4.

64. A further justification of this chiastic reading can be found in the fact that the servant poem is bracketed by passages dealing with the restored Jerusalem: 51:17-53:12 and ch.54, which would expand the chiasm to ABCDC'B'A' where A and A' would correspond to these sections on the new Jerusalem. In that case, the lengthy passage 51:17-54:17 in which the new Jerusalem is addressed would conclude the "Book of the Consolation of Israel" that was inaugurated with an address to the old Jerusalem about to be redeemed. Notice the similarity between 40:9 and 52:7.

65. Compare with Is 6:1 where the same verbs *rum* and *nissa'* appear.

fortunes will be widely known, for the radical and apparently inexplicable change in his fortunes will trigger astonishment among the nations.[66]

And if the nations are bewildered at this, it is nothing to Israel's bewilderment. The servant's peers not only witness the same incomprehensible turn of events (53:1-3) but also are faced with the discovery that his suffering is for their sake; he endures it as a sacrificial lamb for their iniquities (vv.4-6). As for the servant himself, he willingly goes to his death without even opening his mouth (vv.7-9), even though his sentence is the verdict of an oppressive, unjust human *mišpat* (v.8a).

After relating the servant's tragic "end," the text then reveals that his sorrows were deliberately orchestrated by God (v.10a). What's more, the success of God's purpose in setting up these events depends wholly on the servant's reaction to it—only if he willingly, unquestioningly accepts God's plan for him will it succeed (v.10b and d).[67] The servant must quietly go to his fate of suffering and death as a sacrificial lamb, an offering for sin (vv.7, 10). Should he lend a deaf ear to God or resist his command—as his servant Israel has done so many times—then the divine purpose would not prosper.

The strength of the text's emphasis on the servant's implicit obedience to God's will can be seen in the way the final announcement of his glorification in v.12a is bracketed by v.11b and

66. The phrase "many nations" actually means "all nations" here. The Hebrew *rabbim* (many) often bears the meaning "as many as there are," i.e., "all." That it does in the present context can be gathered from the parallel between "all" in 53:6 and "many" in vv.11 and 12. See also Is 2:2-3 where "all the nations" parallels "many peoples."

67. Notice the *'im* (if) at the beginning of v.10b: "*if* he makes himself an offering for sin, he shall see his offspring, he shall prolong his days; the will of the Lord shall prosper in his hand." (v.10bcd) The Hebrew *'im* can also be translated "when," as it is in RSV, but the sense is the same: the servant must "make himself" (i.e., it must be his own doing) an offering before the Lord's purpose can prosper. In v.10d the implication of v.10b is made explicit: the "prosperity" (success) of the "will of the Lord" is "in his hand" (in his power; under his control).

v.12bc which speak of his voluntary sacrifice. A causal relationship between the voluntary sacrifice and the glorification is asserted through an awkward syntactical construction that makes v.12a the result of both what precedes it and what follows it:

> by his knowledge shall the righteous one, my servant,
>> make many to be accounted righteous;
>> and he shall bear their iniquities. (v.11b)
>
> *Therefore* I will divide him a portion with the great,
>> and he shall divide the spoil with the strong; (v.12a)
>
> *because* he poured out his soul to death,
>> and was numbered with the transgressors, (v.12b)
>
> yet he bore the sin of many,
>> and made intercession for the transgressors. (v.12c)

The servant's stubbornly consistent silence gives God free rein to do what he alone can do: vindicate with his *mišpat* the one declared guilty by human *mišpat*; establish glory amid shame and rejection; and grant life where there is death. In contrast to Israel's habitual disobedience "forcing" the Lord's hand,[68] through the servant's perfect obedience God is now given the opportunity to do things completely his way, without interference, from beginning to end.

In other words, this servant would offer God an absolutely obstruction-free "void" within the realm of the human world and history, that he may act as the "Creator ex nihilo" of a new world, his world, the way he wants it; where the impossible is daily bread and where the present reality, in which the barren one cannot possibly conceive, gives way to one where "the children of the barren one are more than those of the one that is married" (54:1). Thus, Second Isaiah conceived the impossible dream: a human clay for God the potter. With earthen clay, in the beginning God made humans, but they rebelled and wrecked his world; with Second Isaiah's human clay, God will be able to implant the new "heavenly" Jerusalem (ch.54) at the heart of the world wreckage.

---

68. See comments on Ezek 20.

The Identity of the Servant of the Poems

Thus, the question, "Whom did Second Isaiah have in mind when speaking of the servant?" is unanswerable if one is expecting in reply the name of a specific person. Rather, the servant is a wishful thought on the prophet's part, an eschatological vision, as it were—which, if or when realized, will "take flesh."[69] The eschatological setting against which the servant is cast makes him the ultimate "end-time" person though whom God will enact his unhindered reign in this world.

Consequently, although Second Isaiah himself did not have a specific individual in mind, it remains for the reader to decide if and in whom his prophecy is fulfilled. For the reader of these poems, then, the servant is someone who lies in the future—until the reader himself decides to recognize, acknowledge, and confess someone as the servant. No other way is possible since the servant himself is essentially silent and thus no answer can be expected from him. If this seems problematic, it can't be helped; one must remember that the servant is part and parcel of the prophetic word of the poems, which are in turn part and parcel of Second Isaiah's entire message—and that message is itself characterized as being anything but simple, straightforward, and easy to understand:

> For my thoughts are not your thoughts, neither are your ways my ways, says the Lord. For as the heavens are higher than the earth, so are my ways higher than your ways and my thoughts than your thoughts. For as the rain and the snow come down from heaven, and return not thither but water the earth, making it bring forth and sprout, giving seed to the sower and bread to the eater, so shall my word that goes forth from my mouth; it shall not return to me empty, but it shall accomplish that which I purpose, and prosper in the thing for which I sent it. (55:8-11)[70]

69. "If" from a human perspective, "when" from God's perspective.

70. Notice the same idea of God's purpose or will "prospering," which we find in 53:10d in reference to the servant. The Hebrew behind "purpose" here and "will" in 53:10d is the same word (here in the verbal form *hapasti* and there in the nominal form *hepes*). Likewise, the words for "prosper" here and in v.10d are just different

Nevertheless, the reader is called upon to obey God's word, if not to understand it totally. This passage is embedded within an appeal to the (willfully deaf) servant, Israel, to "hearken," "incline the ear," and "hear," so that "your soul may live" (55:2-3).[71] The result of such obedient listening would be Israel's "glorification" by the Lord and transformation into a refuge for "the nations" (v.5).[72] One can only conclude that Second Isaiah already presupposes his future readers' difficulties in identifying the servant: the "advent" of the Lord's servant will have as its corollary a challenge to Israel to "incline the ear" and acknowledge that the Lord's design did prosper in the servant's hand; only then will God's *mišpat* be realized in the eyes of the nations, who will then flock to the "new" Jerusalem.

In the history of Israel after Second Isaiah's day, this did happen once—and only once—when a number of Jews in 1st century A.D. Palestine confessed that God's design was realized in Jesus of Nazareth, who was put to a shameful death and afterward was vindicated in glory. That community of Jewish "believers" in Jesus as the Lord's eschatological servant adopted the same verb "evangelize" *(bisser-evangelizomai)* with which Second Isaiah characterized his entire message as "good news."[73] Thus, Second Isaiah's prophetic word requiring faith in the Lord's final *mišpat* finds its realization in another word, the apostolic word, which uses the prophetic vocabulary and also requires faith that the Lord did implement his final *mišpat*. The Apostle Paul characterizes this process as a movement *ek pisteos eis pistin* (from [one stand of] faith to [another stand of] faith; Rom 1:17). The faith he has in mind here is in one and the same God whose "*gospel* he promised

forms of the same verb (perfect *hisliah*, imperfect *yislah*).

71. Contrast with 53:12 where the servant's obedience leads him to "pour out his soul to death" for the sake of his peers' iniquities and sins (vv.11-12).

72. Compare with the second poem (49:1-6) where the Lord will be "glorified" in his servant, the "light to the nations."

73. It brackets the entire "Book of Consolation" (see 40:9; 52:7).

beforehand through his prophets in the holy scriptures,[74] concerning his Son...designated as Son of God in power according to
the Spirit of holiness by his resurrection from the dead (Rom
1:1-4). It is this "gospel" that is "the power of God for salvation to
every one who has faith, to the Jew first and also to the Greek.[75]
For in it the righteousness [i.e., *mišpat*] of God is revealed *ek
pisteos eis pistin.*" (Rom 1:16-17) The Jew is first in that he is
already bound by the prophetic scripture requiring faith in the
promised divine word, whereas the Gentile begins by acknow-
ledging the prophetic scripture as *divine word* entailing a promise.
Both Jew and Gentile, however, are on a par in that they are
required to *believe* that the promised divine word was *fulfilled* in
Jesus the Christ.

74. The intimate connection between the word of promise and the gospel as word of
    fulfillment of that promise, is evidenced by the prominence of Second Isaiah in
    Paul's mind when he speaks of the "mechanism" of the apostolic proclamation and
    its reception further in the same epistle (Rom 10:17). Compare that text especially
    with 52:7 and 53:1, i.e., the fourth servant poem and its immediate context.
75. Recall the comments above on 55:2-5, where Israel is called to "hear" in order that
    it may itself "live" and then become a refuge for "the nations."

IV

The Post-Exilic Period

13

The Second Scripture

The Babylonian exiles' optimistic hopes for better treatment under Cyrus were realized. Not only did the new conqueror allow them to return to the lands from which the previous conqueror had taken them, he even permitted them to undertake a degree of self-government. Given this opportunity, it was not long before a group of Judahite exiles headed home. They were led by members of what used to be the Jerusalem priesthood, which, in the absence of a king, had taken over the banner of leadership among the exiles.[1] Since one of the priests' main interests was naturally to resume services in the Jerusalem temple of the Lord, before quitting Babylon they sought and successfully procured an edict from Cyrus allowing the rebuilding of the temple.[2] Upon their arrival in Judah, then, one of the first orders of business was to begin that task. Fortunately for the returnees, recruiting local laborers for such an ambitious undertaking was not difficult because the temple was destined to become the essential symbol of Judah as a revived political entity; in the absence of an earthly king's palace administration, the temple of the heavenly King would be the rallying center of the new Persian province of Judah. However, whether due to the complacency of the Jewish community or to Samaritan obstruction,[3] the reconstruction effort soon lagged. The grand project then lay dormant until the second year of Darius I's reign (520 B.C.), when it was resumed under the impetus of two prophets, Haggai and Zechariah.[4]

1. See vol.1, p.122 and introductory remarks on Ezekiel.
2. See Ezra 1:1-4; 6:1-5. See also 2 Chr 36:22-23.
3. See Hag 1:1-11; Ezra 4.
4. See Ezra 5:1-2; Hag 1:1-11; Zech 1:1.

Haggai and Zechariah

The oracles of Haggai and Zechariah deal with the situation in Jerusalem between 520 and 518 B.C.[5] Like the rest of the prophetic literature, both of the canonical books are edited works, but the latter is a special case. It is composed of two disparate sections, chs.1-8 containing the words of Zechariah himself and chs.9-14 coming from a later period. The appended material is called Second Zechariah and will be discussed below.[6]

As for the first section, it can be further subdivided into relatively independent parts. The introductory paragraph 1:1-6 does not seem to have any connection with the following 1:7-6:15, a series of visions introduced with a single date (1:7). Moreover, while the prophetic books typically include a prophet's lineage along with his name only in a book's introduction,[7] here the text identifies Zechariah in this way at the beginning of both sections (in 1:1 and 1:7). We saw a similar phenomenon in Is 1:1 and 2:1, and in each case it signifies the work of an editor combining at least two originally independent sets of oracles. In this case it appears that Zech 1:1-6 was placed where it is to serve as a general introduction to the compilation of Zech chs.1-8 and chs.9-14 into one work. It is in fact an appropriate introduction to a work containing writings spanning multiple generations, since it emphasizes the perennial validity of God's prophetic word, which outlives many generations of human beings.[8]

Nevertheless, it is noteworthy that the date given to the introductory oracle (1:1-6) falls between that of the second and third oracles in Haggai (2:1, 10), whereas Zech 1:7 and 7:1 are both dated after the fourth oracle (Hag 2:20). The chronological link

5. Hag 1:1; 2:1; 2:10; Zech 1:1; 1:7; 7:1.
6. For a discussion on the phenomenon of multiple sections in prophetic books and the naming of them, see the introductory comments on the book of Isaiah.
7. As in Jer 1:1; Ezek 1:3; Hos 1:1; Joel 1:1; Jon 1:1; Mic 1:1; Zeph 1:1.
8. See also comments above on Is ch.1 which serves as an introduction to the works of Isaiah, Second Isaiah, and Third Isaiah.

to Haggai's calls to rebuild the temple (1:1-15a and 1:15b-2:9) indicates that such may have been the original intended purpose of Zech 1:1-6 also. The similar threatening tone (compare with Hag 2:15-19), and the fact that the following visions address the restoration of Jerusalem and its temple service, tend to confirm this supposition.

Besides the emphasis on temple reconstruction, an important element in the teachings of both Haggai and Zechariah is the idea that religious and civil authority, while distinct, are on the same level: both treat Joshua, the high priest, and Zerubbabel, the governor of the Judean province, as leaders of equal rank.[9] This is reflective of the post-exilic situation where the Jews formed a body religious, a commonwealth ruled by a *torah* that functioned as a universal authority. In other words, in this treatment of authority figures one witnesses the rise of nascent Judaism as a "religion"[10] along with the rise to prominence of the temple—and Jerusalem as the city of the temple—in post-exilic thought.

Following the lead of Ezekiel, not only did Haggai and Zechariah concentrate on the temple and its service, but they viewed it in a universal, and thus eschatological, perspective. It is telling in this respect that Haggai's second oracle already looks ahead to the end times: "For thus says the Lord of hosts: Once again, in a little while, I will shake the heavens and the earth and the sea and the dry land; and I will shake all nations, so that the treasures of all nations shall come in, and I will fill this house with splendor, says the Lord of hosts...and in this place I will give *šalom* (peace/prosperity), says the Lord of hosts." (2:6-9)[11] Small wonder, then, that the prophecies of Haggai and Zechariah each end with a messianic oracle (2:20-23 and ch.8 respectively), or that the proph-

9. See Hag 1:1, 12, 14; 2:2, 4; Zech 3:1-4:14. Note also that the priestly office is closely connected with the prophetic function in the guidance of the people respecting religious matters (see Zech 7:3).

10. See vol.1, ch.14.

11. See further Hag 2:21-22; Zech 2:13-17.

ecy of Zechariah as a whole (1:7-8:23) is patterned after that of Ezekiel (both cover the entire history of Jerusalem, from its pre-exilic history of sinfulness triggering disaster, up to its glorious end).[12]

Joel and Obadiah

The same view of the eschatological day of the Lord as a day of ultimate divine victory in the "new Jerusalem" can be detected in the prophecy of Joel. However, here it is contrasted with the chastening day of the Lord in 587 when he destroyed "old Jerusalem" for its sins. The book opens with a proleptic picture of a desolate Judah (1:2-13, 16-20), a scenario destined to come true if the call to prayerful repentance (1:14-15) is ignored. Ch.2 repeats this theme, appending yet another fervent appeal to repentance (vv.12-17) to a description of the dreadful upcoming day of the Lord (vv.1-9). Should the appeals meet with a positive response, the outcome will be God's recasting of his day of visitation from one of destruction to one of salvation for Jerusalem (vv.18-27), culminating in a new era (vv.28-32).

Ch.3 builds upon the idea of the new era in a manner reminiscent of Ezek chs.38-39: the reality and permanence of the new "spiritual"[13] order is tested (1-17), with the result being its recognition as God's work of everlasting salvation for his people (18-21).[14] Notice the striking correspondence between the endings of both books: "And the name of the city henceforth shall be, The Lord is there" (Ezek 48:35) vs. "for the Lord dwells in Zion" (Joel 3:21). The universalistic aspect of the Ezekielian eschatological battle (38:1-39:20), however, is rendered in Joel with the traditional pre-exilic terminology according to which "the nations" means the surrounding countries (in this case Tyre, Sidon, and Philistia in 3:4; and Egypt and Edom in 3:19).

12. In which case Zech 1:1-6 is a worthy introduction to 1:7-8:23 as well as to the entire book.

13. Compare the pouring out of the spirit on all flesh (Joel 2:28) with Ezek 37:1-14.

14. Compare 1-17 with Ezek 38-39:20 and 18-21 with Ezek 39:21-29.

Obadiah employs the same language. When speaking of "the day of the Lord" which is "near upon *all the nations*" (v.15), this book specifically identifies Philistia, Gilead, Phoenicia (vv.19-20), and especially Edom (passim). Although the singling out of Edom suggests a less than universal scope, the true character of Obadiah's prophecy can be seen in its final words looking forward to the establishment of David's kingdom in its utopian all-encompassing extent (vv.19-20).[15] The prominence of Edom is due to its "sibling rivalry" with Judah,[16] which seems to have intensified during the post-exilic period. The Edomites had taken advantage of Judah's helplessness in 587 in order to terminate the long-standing Judahite hegemony over them and even grab for themselves some Judahite land;[17] such actions were remembered bitterly by Judah when it re-established itself as a Persian province, and the old feud was reborn.

Jonah

Alongside the view that "the day of the Lord" would be one of victory over and subjugation of the nations, there was in nascent Judaism the line of thought championed by Second Isaiah, especially in his servant poems, whereby the "redeemed" nations are invited into the "new" Jerusalem which is itself "redeemed." Those who espoused the more benign view of the nations' fate also tended to perceive circumcision not as an opportunity for exclusivism and narrow-mindedness but rather as an open invitation to *all* to become "children of Abraham."[18] The book of Jonah represents one example of this tendency to interpret Yahweh's universality in an inclusivistic light. When one considers the fact that all other Old Testament prophets were commissioned either

15. A similar phenomenon can be found in Is 34, which is an oracle against Edom sandwiched between chs.33 and 35 that speak of the eschatological restoration of Jerusalem.

16. Edom/Esau is the brother of Israel/Jacob (v.10). See Gen 27; 32-33.

17. See 2 Sam 8:13-14//1 Chr 18:12-13. This situation may well be reflected in the tendential rendering of Joel 3:19.

18. See vol.1, ch.12.

to Israel or Judah, this book is conspicuously "unorthodox" in the sense that it presents the Israelite prophet Jonah[19] with a mission not just to an outsider but to none other than Nineveh, Israel's archenemy. Furthermore, the mission is not to condemn Nineveh but to urge the sinful city to repent and thereby avoid its punishment! That the Israelite Jonah would desperately want to turn down such an unpleasant commission (ch.1) is quite understandable. What makes the book even more "unorthodox" is the fact that it is Jonah himself, God's prophet, who in the end is upbraided rather than the sinful Ninevites—again a unique case in the prophetic literature. The message of the book is crystal clear: the Lord is definitely the one, universal God, and consequently it is not only Israel and Judah who constitute his people. His message is the same to those outside those kingdoms as it is to those within them: he calls all to salvation through repentance.

"God's Rule/Kingdom" and Apocalypticism

The hopes many Jews laid on the post-exilic theocracy in the Persian province of Judah were shattered when the priestly leadership eventually proved to be as oppressive as the pre-exilic kingly administration. Disappointment in this post-exilic new Jerusalem led the poor and the oppressed to begin hoping for a better future not dependent on any human commonwealth but rather based on the direct intervention by the divine King himself to assert his rule on earth. The movement borne of these hopes is known as apocalyptic, its mindset apocalypticism, and its books "apocalypses" or "revelations." The word comes from the Greek verb *apokalypto* meaning "to unveil, reveal." Apocalyptic books typically present God as the unequivocal master of human destiny who chooses to "reveal" to his special messengers the unfolding of future events, especially those related to

19. The tradition preserved in 2 Kg 14:25 will have provided the author of the book of Jonah with the name Jonah, son of Amittai. The latter was active during the reign of Jeroboam II who ruled the kingdom of Israel between 783 and 743 B.C., i.e., in the heyday of Nineveh.

his ultimate intervention to establish his de facto rule in the universe. The best-known example is the New Testament book of "Revelation" or "Apocalypse."

According to the apocalyptic vision of things the establishment of the Lord as the ruling King takes place in his city, Jerusalem. Hence, the earliest such writings arose from circles critical of the ruling Jerusalemite priesthood. But in order for such writings to survive to our time, those circles also had to be influential enough to have their teachings integrated into the main literature of nascent Judaism, which was in the hands of the Jerusalem temple administration. Only one group meets these paradoxical requirements: the Levites.[20]

For their first efforts, the budding apocalypticists could not be expected to write a book and circulate it on their own authority. Rather, they would want to attach it to an existing authority. Which one? Keep in mind that the promises of hope for divine vindication were mainly for the poor and oppressed, as had always been the case in the prophetic tradition. That being the case, a strong rallying point for the new message of the "apocalyptic" circles was easily found in the person of the Second Isaianic servant, the very image of one afflicted by his peers yet eventually vindicated and glorified by God. And consequently, the "apocalyptic" writings found a ready home within the Isaianic writings.

Third Isaiah

What may be considered as the earliest "apocalypse" occurs in Is chs.24-27. This long passage speaking of the Lord's ultimate epiphany in glory and culminating with the restoration of Israel at Jerusalem (27:12-13) was deliberately inserted into a context of invective against the nations, the traditional enemies of Israel and Judah.[21]

20. See vol.1, ch.15.
21. It follows the oracles against the nations in chs.13-23 and precedes a renewed invective against them in chs.28-32.

However, the bulk of the post-exilic "Isaianic" material was appended to the Isaianic "Book of Consolation" and became what is now known in scholarship as Third or Trito-Isaiah (chs.56-66). The reader will easily notice that the largest portion of these writings address the injustice prevailing in post-exilic Jerusalem and criticize, therefore, those in positions of leadership (56:10-58:12; 63:7-64:11; 65:1-66:17). The hopelessness of the situation as felt by the author of this text is reflected in the fact that it requires a prophet/savior along the lines of the Second Isaianic servant to proclaim its end:

> The Spirit of the Lord is upon me, because the Lord has anointed me to bring good tidings to the afflicted; he has sent me to bind up the brokenhearted, to proclaim liberty to the captives, and the opening of the prison to those who are bound; to proclaim the year of the Lord's favor, and the day of vengeance of our God; to comfort all who mourn; to grant to those who mourn in Zion—to give them a garland instead of ashes, the oil of gladness instead of mourning, the mantle of praise instead of a faint spirit; that they may be called oaks of righteousness, the planting of the Lord, that he may be glorified. (61:1-3)

Like the servant, this anointed one has as his goal God's glorification. His mission, however, is not realized through his own affliction within Israel, but rather by bearing the good tidings of the end of their affliction to those who are oppressed in Jerusalem. "Good news for Jerusalem" is a key point for Third Isaiah and is expressed by means of the same verb *bisser* (to proclaim good news) used by Second Isaiah when speaking of God's eschatological rule in Jerusalem.[22]

On the other hand, their interest in the poor and oppressed within the Persian province of Judah gave the apocalyptic writings a flavor similar to that of the pre-exilic prophets who castigated the Israelite and Judahite leadership. Alongside the stress on Israel as a totality which this literature shared with the hopeful eschatol-

---

22. Is 40:9; 52:7. It turns up again in Third Isaiah in 60:6 (there translated just "proclaim" in RSV).

ogy of Jeremiah, Ezekiel, and Second Isaiah, it accorded equal importance to the righteous individual within Israel. And here in Third Isaiah, that emphasis on the individual extends even to the "new Jerusalem" (56:2; 57:1-2; 58:6-10; 60:21; 66:2b).

The Book of Isaiah

The result of all the additions and editorial work on the book of Isaiah is a finished product which is a kind of a masterpiece compendium of the whole "story of Israel" (i.e., Israel and Judah) and its relationship with its God, a story of continual faithlessness on the part of Israel and equally unrelenting faithfulness on the Lord's part.[23] It may also be viewed as a whole series of stories following one repeated pattern, according to which the people through their rebellions try to put an end to the story, but God, through his prophet(s), always has the last word. Considering how this pattern is consistent right up to the ultimate end of the story as a whole, the book of Isaiah can be viewed as the *entire* "story of God's word" within the realm of *all* human history from beginning to end.[24] This universal "story" is presented more specifically as the history of the city of Jerusalem from its beginnings to its end as the "new" Jerusalem.[25] Yet the city is always viewed from the perspective of the end, as we see already in Isaiah's opening "vision" describing the eschatological Jerusalem where God's *šalom* (peace) is established and to which all the nations flock (2:1-4).

The view of the city as microcosm fits well with the Isaianic school's conviction that Jerusalem is the city of the Lord, the God of the beginning and the end, the One who is the same and as

23. The interesting hymn in Is 63:7-64:14 presents this theme in a nutshell.
24. Notice the repeated stress on the beginnings and the end, and more often one in conjunction with the other, especially in Second Isaiah: 40:21; 41:4, 26; 44:6-8; 46:9-11; 48:12-13. See also 40:12, 25-28; 44:24-28; 45:18-19; 51:9-11; these speak of creation and thus implicitly of beginnings.
25. On the city as a microcosm, see vol.1, pp.12 and 48.

glorious and majestic in his first theophany (2:6-22) as he is every subsequent time up to the last and eternal one. However—and this too is made clear right from the beginning in the same text presenting the first epiphany (2:6-22)—God's coming in glory is double-edged in the sense that it judges as well as saves. The bright and luminous day of victory of the Lord is at the same time a dark day of terror:

> O house of Jacob, come, let us walk in the light of the Lord. For thou hast rejected thy people, the house of Jacob, because...their land is filled with silver and gold, and there is no end to their treasures; their land is filled with horses, and there is no end to their chariots. Their land is filled with idols; they bow down to the work of their hands, to what their own fingers have made. So man is humbled, and men are brought low—forgive them not! Enter into the rock, and hide in the dust from before the terror of the Lord, and from the glory of his majesty. The haughty looks of man shall be brought low, and the pride of men shall be humbled; and the Lord alone will be exalted in that day...In that day men will cast forth their idols of silver and their idols of gold, which they made for themselves to worship, to the moles and to the bats, to enter the caverns of the rocks and the clefts of the cliffs, from before the terror of the Lord, and from the glory of his majesty, when he rises to terrify the earth. (2:5-11, 20-21)

This is typical of the divine epiphanies: they are all connected with Jerusalem and entail judgment as well as salvation, including those that take place through the Second Isaianic servant and the one that takes place in the post-exilic restored Jerusalem.

Micah

Historically, the Isaianic "story of Jerusalem" begins with the Assyrian threat in 701 B.C. under Hezekiah. Since the siege by Sennacherib's armies was eventually lifted, Isaiah's words of indictment against Jerusalem (ch.8) were not viewed as having been realized until the catastrophe of 587. Later came Second Isaiah with his message of salvation, and finally Third Isaiah with his indictment of post-exilic restored Jerusalem and hopeful anticipation of the eschatological Jerusalem. The result is that the shape of the canonical book of Isaiah reflects two succeeding "waves" of divine condemnation followed by divine salvation.

The book of Micah reflects the same "two-wave" pattern. Since Micah was a contemporary of Isaiah, and like him a messenger to Judah, his message had to be edited along the same lines in order to make it relevant within nascent Judaism. It contains an initial message of condemnation (chs.1-3) followed by promises of salvation (chs.4-5), then another indictment (6:1-7:7) followed by a final message of hope for eschatological restoration (7:8-20). A clear indication of the editorial process by which Micah was likened to Isaiah can be detected in the similar emphasis on individual righteousness in Mic 6:1-7:7 (especially 6:6-8; 7:1-7) compared to Third Isaiah.

Second Zechariah and Malachi

These two works strongly reflect the same concerns as those of Third Isaiah and may even have originated in circles akin to, if not the same as, those that produced the latter. Besides being thoroughly apocalyptic in character, Second Zechariah contains passages that betray the interests of the post-exilic Levites who were behind the emerging "apocalyptic" literary genre.[26] Such evidence includes: (a) criticism of the post-exilic priestly leadership spoken of as pastors (10:2; 11:4-17; 13:7-9) and prophets (13:2-6); (b) the idea that the Lord values his "lesser servants" as highly as the Jerusalemite leadership (12:7-8); and, in conjunction with the preceding, (c) a stress on individual righteousness to the degree that a purge of the unrighteous ones from within Israel is expected (13:8-9; 14:2).

In its turn, Malachi also displays a series of traits indicative of the late post-exilic period:

---

26. See above on the Levites' involvement in apocalypticism. The apocalyptic character of Second Zechariah is most readily apparent in its opening and ending chapters (9 and 14).

1) The feeling of enmity toward Edom (1:2-5).

2) An unusually lengthy indictment levelled against priests (1:6-2:9).

3) Condemnation of divorces and "mixed" marriages (2:10-16). While this theme closely parallels what we find in Ezra 9-10, here it seems to be aimed primarily at the priests, which would make it a continuation of the previous passage: (a) Judah is said to have "profaned the sanctuary of the Lord" (v.11); (b) among the guilty is "the one who brings an offering to the Lord of hosts" (v.12); (c) the defendants are accused in these words: "You cover the Lord's altar with tears, with weeping and groaning because he no longer regards the offering or accepts it with favor at your hands" (v.13);[27] (d) the divorced wife is referred to as "your wife by *covenant*" (v.14) which recalls the *"covenant* of Levi" in 2:4 and 8; and (e) the following section dealing with the day of the Lord (2:17-3:5) both addresses the priests and contains features similar to some found in 2:10-16.[28]

4) The announcement that the Lord will personally take action in order to correct the evil situation obtaining in Jerusalem (2:17-3:5). That this section addresses a priesthood gone astray can be gathered from the following: (a) those who "weary the Lord" do so with an ironic statement mimicking a priestly *torah*: "Every one who does evil is good in the sight of the Lord" (v.17); (b) the Lord or the messenger of the covenant "will purify the *sons of Levi* and refine them till they present right offerings to the Lord.[29] Then the offering of Judah and Jerusalem will be pleasing to the Lord" (vv.3-4).

5) The last section of the book announces that the day of the Lord will divide between the righteous and the wicked and that only the former will be vindicated (3:13-4:3).[30]

27. Notice that 1:6-14 deals specifically with the priestly offering, and this seems to repeat that theme.

28. Compare 2:12-13 with 3:3, and talk of "Judah and Jerusalem" in 2:11 with 3:4.

29. This recalls the mention of Levi in 2:4 and 8.

30. The role of 4:4 and 4:5-6 as appendices to the book's text is discussed below.

The Prophetic Literature and the "Second Scripture"

The final arrangement of the Second Zechariah writings into two parts (chs.9-10 and 12-14), each entitled with the same term *massa'* (oracle) found at the head of the book of Malachi, seems to betray an editorial hand and suggests that the three oracles were meant to be read as an interrelated group. Notice how *massa'* in Zech 9:1 serves as the sole title of chs.9-10; the following phrase, "the word of the Lord," is part of the oracle itself rather than a title.[31] But in Zech 12:1 and Mal 1:1 the expression "the word of the Lord" after *massa'* is not part of the text but is itself a title.[32] The fact that *massa'* in the second two instances is superfluous indicates it must be an editorial addition, apparently intended to mimic Zech 9:1.[33] And that in turn tells us that Zech chs.9-10, Zech chs.12-14, and Malachi were meant to be read as a trilogy.

This trilogy's perspective parallels Third Isaiah's, and those who preserved it as scripture found a similar home for it. The prophecy of Third Isaiah, critical of the post-exilic Jerusalem which had been hailed by Second Isaiah as the "new Jerusalem," was appended to Second Isaiah. Likewise this trilogy: critical of the same post-exilic Jerusalem and looking ahead for the eschatological one, it offered an appropriate counterpoint to the prophecies of Zechariah, whose work ended with a chapter (eight) viewing the post-exilic Jerusalem with its new temple as the eschatological city of God.

Thus, by the time the canon of the prophetic writings was brought to a close, the scroll of the so-called "minor prophets"[34]

31. Other instances of *massa'* acting as a title: Is 13:1; 15:1; 17:1; 19:1; 21:1, 11, 13; 22:1; 23:1; Nah 1:1; Hab 1:1.
32. RSV prints "Oracle" as a title for Zech 9:1 and 12:1 but not for Mal 1:1, which it renders "The oracle of the word of the Lord ..." The latter is a possible translation, but the Hebrew in all three cases is identical. Whether one considers *massa'* to be separate or not, the fact remains that it is superfluous and that the phrase beginning "the word of the Lord" can stand alone as the title.
33. Duality of title is a sure sign of editorial work; see other examples in Ezek 1:1-3; Nah 1:1.
34. The writings of the "minor prophets" were included in one scroll or book similar in size to each of the scrolls of the three "major prophets" (Isaiah, Ezekiel, and

and the scroll of Isaiah had similar endings. In fact, the similarity goes beyond their endings: both scrolls decry the sins of both pre-exilic and post-exilic Jerusalem and look ahead to the eschatological Jerusalem. As for Ezekiel, that scroll was substantial and already ended with a grandiose vision of the "new temple" in the restored Jerusalem; it did not need any major editing, especially since the eschatological test of chs.38-39[35] effectively ruled out any premature rejoicing at the arrival of the eschatological age. Jeremiah was somewhat harder to handle since his prophecies were both totally pre-exilic (like Isaiah's) and long enough to fill a scroll (unlike Is 1-39).[36] But there was room for minimal editing, and that took the form of an appendix (ch.52) parallelling the optimistic ending of the Deuteronomistic History (Deut 24:18-25:30).[37]

If, then, the editing of the prophetic books was oriented not only toward individual prophetic books but also toward scrolls as a whole, one might expect to find evidence of an editorial "finale" to the scroll of the twelve minor prophets. And indeed one does. At the end of the trilogy formed by Second Zechariah and Malachi stand two more or less independent appendices, the first of which reads, "Remember the law of my servant Moses, the statutes and ordinances that I commanded him at Horeb for all Israel" (Mal 4:4); and the second: "Behold, I will send you Elijah the prophet before the great and terrible day of the Lord comes. And he will turn the hearts of fathers to their children and the hearts of children to their fathers, lest I come and smite the land with a curse." (Mal 4:5-6) Both are replete with Deuteronomic vocabulary:

1) The expressions "law of Moses," "Moses, the Lord's servant,"

Jeremiah). This one scroll was known in the Septuagint as the *Dodekapropheton* (the twelve prophets). It goes without saying that the terms "minor" and "major," when speaking of the prophets, refer solely to the size of the writing attributed to each, not to their relative importance.

35. See above on Ezekiel.
36. It may well be that more of his sayings were preserved because he had a personal scribe in his disciple Baruch.
37. See vol.1, pp.117-8.

"statutes and ordinances that the Lord commanded," "all Israel," and the reference to the Holy Mountain as Horeb instead of Sinai, are typical of Deuteronomy and the Deuteronomistic History.[38]

2) Besides his mention here the prophet Elijah appears virtually[39] only in 1 Kg 17-2 Kg 10, i.e., in the literary clusters or cycles dedicated to him (1 Kg 17-2 Kg 1) and to his disciple Elisha (2 Kg 2-13), which are part of the Deuteronomistic History.

3) The use of the term "heart" in conjunction with unequivocal allegiance to the Lord is a trademark of Deuteronomy. Although here the allegiance referred to is ostensibly between fathers and children, that too is Deuteronomic: an essential aspect of the Deuteronomic law was the duty of fathers to hand it down to their children, and that of children to hearken to it and hand it down, in their turn, to their own children. See the confluence of "heart," "fathers," and "children" in such important texts as the introduction (6:4-9) and conclusion (11:18-32) of Moses' comments on the Decalogue.

4) The curse as the alternative to the blessing is a recurrent theme in both D and DH. The conclusion to Moses' comments on the Decalogue in Deut 11:18-32 not only combines "heart," "fathers," and "children," but also conveys the promise of a blessing and the threat of a curse in the land of Israel's dwelling. The same combination serves as the main theme of the book of Joshua, the first book in the Deuteronomistic History.

From this study of the two appendices in Mal 4:4-6 it is evident that their purpose is to bring to completion the "second scripture" by harking back to Deuteronomy, the last book of the *torah,* the "first scripture" of nascent Judaism. Hence the traditional expression *torah un^ebi'im / ho nomos kai hoi prophetai* (the

38. DH includes Joshua through 2 Kings; see vol.1, pp.89-93.

39. The "letter" from the prophet Elijah to Jehoram, referred to in 2 Chr 21:12, is obviously artificial. The author's intention is to include the reigning house in Judah under the same threat leveled by Elijah against the ruling house (of Ahab) in Israel, the common sin being that of idolatry (v.13; also v.6). The link between Jehoram and Ahab lay in that the former was the latter's son-in-law (v.6).

law and the prophets) to speak of scripture as a whole.[40] However, no editor would have wanted to close the scroll of the "minor prophets" with an "incomplete" or "imperfect" number of prophets; what was needed was a number like 12, the traditional number expressing the fullness and completeness appropriate to "all Israel" (Mal 4:4) with its 12 tribes. To do that, the editor made the last part of the trilogy mentioned above into a separate book. The name the editor gave this new "book," *mal'aki*, literally means "my messenger" and no doubt refers to the Lord's messenger of Mal 3:1 who "prepares the way before him" and whom the editor made into Elijah, the eschatological forerunner of the Lord's day (4:5). This new "book" ending the scroll of the "minor prophets" is in fact a *massa'* (oracle) entirely dedicated to the announcement of "the Day of the Lord" (3:2, 17; 4:1, 3), a notion fundamental to all of the prophetic literature, including "Malachi" himself.

The importance of this "day," then, can hardly be overestimated. It consistently conveys a two-sided message to the reader of these texts, representing at once condemnation and salvation. The catastrophic closing of the "former prophets" (2 Kg ch.25), when compared with its glorious opening (the book of Joshua), is a constant reminder of the dark side of this reality. A "prophetic" word preceding the Lord's "last" Day and giving fair warning of it is, therefore, an absolute necessity. And God himself, according to Malachi, already had this in mind when he decided to take up to himself one of the *prophets,* Elijah (2 Kg 2:1-13), in order to save him for that "last" mission (4:5-6). The mention of Elijah at the end of the "second scripture," understood as the writings of and about the prophets, made out of him in the tradition of nascent Judaism the representative of the prophets in the same way that Moses had been viewed as the representative of the *torah.*[41] Hence, and in parallel with the expression "the law and the

40. See Mt 5:17; 7:12; 11:13; Lk 16:16.

41. The honor was given him especially by his Deuteronomic "testament" at the end of the "first scripture."

prophets," came about the traditional coupling of Moses and Elijah.[42]

42. See Mt 17:3, 4//Mk 9:4, 5//Lk 9:30, 33.

14

Daniel

The Septuagint places the book of Daniel right after Ezekiel, thereby suggesting that Daniel is to be considered the fourth "major prophet." In the Hebrew Old Testament, however, the book's location is toward the end of the "third scripture" known as $k^e tubim$ (the writings).[1] Its presence in that section rather than among the prophets indicates either its late provenance or its late acceptance into the Jewish scriptures, since the canon of the $k^e tubim$ remained open until the end of the first century A.D., long after the "second scripture" of prophetic books reached completion sometime between the fifth and third centuries B.C. If it was actually published early enough for inclusion in the prophetic canon, but was not, then this would be evidence that it simply was not considered to be a prophetic book. But that does not jibe with the fact that the Septuagint did include it with the prophets; and besides, the exilic and post-exilic prophetic literature does contain apocalyptic material such as Daniel in addition to strictly prophetic utterances. The most likely conclusion is that Daniel was written at a relatively late date, not just accepted into the canon late.

The book is best understood if read as a product of apocalypticism in its heyday. The apocalyptic mindset viewed history as totally controlled by God, notwithstanding any appearances to the contrary. Its writings presented history as unfolding according to a pattern of succeeding periods of *human* rule over the destiny of the universe, the last of which is followed by the inauguration of everlasting *divine* rule. Usually the number of these historical

1. The "writings" are Psalms, Job, Proverbs, Ruth, Song of Songs, Ecclesiastes, Lamentations, Esther, Daniel, Ezra, Nehemiah, and 1 and 2 Chronicles, in that order.

periods is a "full" or "complete" one: four, seven, ten, or twelve.[2] This "fullness" or "completeness" is indicative of God's absolute control over history at every point in its development and therefore his foreknowledge of these periods. That in turn gives him the ability to convey this knowledge ahead of time to whichever seers he chooses, usually through visions whose meaning is "revealed" by means of divine intermediaries. The seer is asked to commit God's *apokalypsis* (revelation) into writing and seal it until the opportune moment, which is usually the last days of the last period of human rule, i.e., just before the eschatological divine intervention.

Due to the apparent absence of God in the management of world affairs, those who believe in him and his ultimate power to control world destiny will see their faith tested until it is vindicated by God himself who will intervene to save miraculously those who witness for him. Not so, however, for those believers who live at the threshold of the period "foreseen"[3] by the apocalypse's protagonist as the end-time leading up to God's open intervention. The nearness of the eschatological age may rule out intermediate, individual miracles. For those living in the last days of human rule, allegiance to God in opposition to human authority will provoke persecution, including physical punishment and even death. Those who maintain unswerving loyalty to God in the face of such persecution are praised as witnesses to him, persevering unto death being the ultimate act of witnessing (hence the English "martyrs," from *martyres* meaning "witnesses").

Consequently, one of the main purposes of apocalyptic writings is to strengthen the faithful in their affliction and exhort them to "persevere until the end." They must realize that *their* end—i.e., their death under persecution—may well come before *the* end. But if that happens, they will nevertheless be vindicated

2. The New Testament book of Revelation provides ample evidence for the importance of these numbers in apocalyptic literature.

3. Typically an apocalypse's author attempts to make it sound as though it was written in a previous age, forecasting as if they were future events things actually happening in the present for the book's author.

even *beyond* death since the divine ruler is also the universal creator who can just as well restore them as create them. The same One who was able to bring about existence where there was none, is able to bring about life from the realm of death, i.e., to resurrect the dead. It is no wonder that this kind of vindication came to be viewed as a safer bet than miraculous immediate salvation: the latter leaves the one saved still within the reach of evil human rulers, whereas the former takes place in the eschatological realm of God's rule where the righteous "shall shine as the stars in heaven," beyond reach of any malicious hand.

The Structure of Daniel

In the Hebrew Old Testament Daniel may be divided into two parts of six chapters each. Chs.1-6 introduce Daniel the seer as a true witness of God and thus as a worthy example for the readers, while chs.7-12 deal more specifically with the vision concerning the difficult times in which the author and the intended readers actually live.

The introduction (1:1-2) sets the Daniel story against the background of the fall of Judah, in order to encourage the reader right from the beginning to look forward to the messianic era of rule according to God's will. The rest of ch.1 extols the faithfulness of Daniel and his companions to God. That quality is implied by their great wisdom (v.4) and is made a matter of public record by their strict adherence to the Jewish dietary rules (v.8).[4] In ch.2 Daniel discovers that history is unfolding according to a four period pattern, after which God's eternal rule is to be inaugurated (vv.31-45). The following three chapters tell how the faith-

4. This explains the choice of "Daniel" as the name of the protagonist. The name occurs only twice elsewhere in the Old Testament (Ezek 14:14; 28:3). In the latter instance it pertains to a man famous for wisdom, in the former to one famous for righteousness. The wisdom tradition had become central in the thought of nascent Judaism, and understandably so; the former acknowledged the oneness of the source of truth, while the latter confessed the oneness of God, whom it naturally considered the source of this truth. See vol.3 (forthcoming).

fulness of Daniel and his companions is tested (ch.3), predict the fall of the first human kingdom (Babylon) under Nebuchadnezzar (ch.4), and tell of that prediction's fulfillment under Nebuchadnezzar's "son"[5] Belshazzar (ch.5). Before continuing to lay out the course of history until its end (chs.7-12), the text offers ch.6 as further evidence that God's revelation to Daniel is true and reliable: it deals with the following human kingdom under Darius the "Mede"[6] in the same way that chs.2-4 did with Nebuchadnezzar. In this manner, the first part of the book already gives hope to readers faced with persecution for witnessing to the Lord, by offering to them as examples Daniel and his companions who were likewise persecuted witnesses, yet were vindicated in the end. As further incentive, the text promises that whereas the characters in the book were allowed to witness God's *ultimate* vindication only in a vision, the readers will experience its full reality—*if* they "persevere until the end" as their ancient predecessors did.

The second part of the book presents visions of the four human kingdoms (chs.7-9), providing much greater detail for the fourth than was offered in ch.2.[7] This reflects the historical period and main interest of the actual author, who was writing immediately before or during the reign of the Seleucid king, Antiochus IV Epiphanes (175-64 B.C.), the terrible "horn."[8] Details about this testing period for Palestinian Jews are given in chs.10-11.[9] Finally, the book concludes with a promise of post-resurrectional (12:2) glory for the faithful, who "shall shine like the stars for ever and ever" (12:3). Yet that vision of the future is nothing new—it is, in fact, none other than the one already revealed at the beginning of the second part (ch.7), as indicated by the reference in 12:1 to the "book" Daniel started to

5. In reality Belshazzar was Nebuchadnezzar's grandson.

6. In reality he was a Persian king.

7. The passages dealing with the fourth vision are 7:23-27; 8:5-14, 19-26; 9:26-27.

8. See 7:24-26; 8:9-11; on the historical background to the book of Daniel, see vol.1, ch.16.

9. The kings of the south and of the north in ch.11 are the Ptolemaic and the Seleucid kings, respectively.

write in 7:1. Here again, the connection is made between Daniel and the readers as between an example and those who are to follow it. Notice that the faithful of 12:3 are referred to as *maskilim* (wise/understanding) just as Daniel and his companions were introduced in 1:4.[10] Finally, the "book" is sealed (12:4, 9) with an invitation to the *maskilim* of the last days to heed and "understand" it (12:10).[11]

The Septuagint Book of Daniel

I indicated earlier, in conjunction with the study of Is 7 and the order of the chapters in Jeremiah, that there was a certain discrepancy between the Hebrew and the Septuagint textual traditions of the Old Testament. In the case of Daniel, the discrepancy takes the form of three additions found in the Septuagint when compared with the Hebrew text: (a) the "prayer of Azariah" and the "song of the three youths" in the furnace, which are inserted between vv.23 and 24 of ch.3; (b) the story of Susanna (ch.13); and (c) the story of Bel and the dragon[12] (ch.14). The latter two are independent of each other as well as of the first 12 chapters but have Daniel as the main personality of the plots.

The Influence of Daniel

The book of Daniel had at least two notable influences evident in the New Testament. The first is its direct bearing on both the content and the vision of the book of Revelation. The second is linked to the "Son of man" figure (ch.7) so prominent in the gospel tradition. This Introduction to the prophetic traditions of the Old Testament is not the place to discuss either of them.[13]

---

10. The importance of this notion of *maskilim* can be gathered from its repeated use at the end of the book (11:33, 35; 12:3, 10) in reference to the *persecuted* faithful.

11. Notice the link between the invitation to understand and the notion of persecution (compare 12:10 with 11:33 and 35), which shows that the intended purpose of the book is to encourage those who are persecuted.

12. Or the story of Bel and the story of the dragon.

13. For a discussion of these issues, see my *Introduction to the New Testament* (forthcoming).

Epilogue

As volume 1 of this series explained, the historical literature of the Old Testament must be approached as a multiplicity of "traditions." The same is true of the prophetic writings. Each of these traditions is linked to the personality of a person who came to be included in an exclusive group known as "the prophets" or "the writing prophets." Being real persons, these prophets appeared at different times in history and were assigned and carried out missions appropriate for their times. Consequently, the messages they proclaimed are also different. We have even found different messages within books, the result of editing intended to make them pertinent for new generations. Thus, there is a "movement," often meandering, from Amos up to Malachi, and, later, Daniel.

This movement must be taken seriously by any student interested in understanding the ultimate source of the prophetic words and traditions, the Lord himself. Since God, through his "word," challenges us and *leads* us to knowledge of him, we must beware of taking the lead ourselves lest we miss the point entirely. All those who open a prophetic book in order to find confirmation of what they thought God was all about might as well save their time and not open it at all; they already know what lies in it! On the other hand, those who open a prophetic book each time as though it were the first and are ready to be both *challenged* and *led* by God's "word" *will* end up understanding it for what it really is—a word that has a "purpose" (Is 55:11), whose ultimate fulfillment lies yet in the future. Those who are granted the privilege of understanding that purpose *may* in the end also be granted the grace of seeing its fulfillment.

What of the Christian view of this word and its fulfillment, the belief that Jesus of Nazareth, who lived and taught in 1st century A.D. Palestine, *is* God's word? Such a confession is meaningless unless one takes seriously the lengthy historical process through which the prophetic *teachings* came to be embedded in the same "second scripture" as the *events* of the Deuteronomistic History, the process by which even "historical" books came to be known as "prophetic." Long before Jesus was born, the name "prior *prophets*" (*nᵉbi'im ri*šonim) ascribed to the Deuteronomistic *History* by nascent Judaism reflected the priority given to prophetic word over historical event in a history viewed as ultimately controlled by God himself. Put otherwise, the prophetic-divine word came to be perceived not merely as taking place within history but rather as triggering and shaping it. Thus, first in the case of the Old Testament prophets, and later—but in the same manner—in the case of the prophet from Nazareth, God's word not only took place in history, but actually "made history," i.e., *created* a history of its own, a history having its beginning in the prophetic-divine word of the Old Testament and its end in the prophetic-divine word of the New Testament. Consequently, in order to get to know the biblical God, the biblical reader must immerse himself in this history where God revealed himself once and for all. And the only way to accomplish such an immersion is through reading this same prophetic-divine word since it is *both* the producer of this history *and* the only record of it available to us. In other words, the fabric of the biblical reality is to become the fabric of the reader's reality, and not vice versa. This is, after all, what circumcision in the Old Testament[1] and baptism in the New Testament, are all about: to enter into the reality of the biblical divine word, and thus into that of the biblical God himself, rather than make them a component of *our* reality.

---

1. See vol 1, pp.129.

Selected Bibliography

General

J. Lindblom, *Prophecy in Ancient Israel,* Oxford, 1962

P. R. Ackroyd, *Exile and Restoration,* OTL [Old Testament Literature series], London, 1968

P. D. Hanson, *The Dawn of Apocalyptic,* Philadelphia, 1975

R. R. Wilson, *Prophecy and Society in Ancient Israel,* Philadlephia, 1980

J. Blenkinsopp, *A History of Prophecy in Israel,* Philadelphia, 1983

K. Koch, *The prophets,* 2 vols, London, 1982-83

T. W. Overholt, *Channels of Prophecy: The Social Dynamics of Prophetic Activity,* Minneapolis, 1989

Commentaries

J. H. Hayes and S. A. Irvine, *Isaiah, The Eighth Century Prophet,* Nashville, 1987

H. Wildberger, *Isaiah 1-12,* Minneapolis, 1991

O. Kaiser, *Isaiah 1-12,* 2nd ed. fully rewritten, Philadelphia, 1983

O. Kaiser, *Isaiah 13-39,* Philadelphia, 1974

C. Westermann, *Isaiah 40-66,* Philadelphia, 1969

R. P. Caroll, *Jeremiah,* OTL, Philadelphia, 1986

W. L. Holladay, *Jeremiah 1 (chs. 1-25)* and *Jeremiah 2 (chs. 26-52),* Hermeneia, Philadelphia, 1986 and 1989

W. Eichrodt, *Ezekiel,* OTL, Philadelphia, 1970

W. Zimmerli, *Ezekiel 1(chs 1-24)* and *Ezekiel 2 (chs. 25-48),* Hermeneia, Philadelphia, 1979 and 1983

N. W. Porteous, *Daniel,* OTL, Philadelphia, 1965

L. F. Hartmann and A. A. Di Lella, *The Book of Daniel,* AB [Anchor Bible series], Garden City, 1978

J. L. Mays, *Hosea,* OTL, Philadelphia, 1969

H. W. Wolff, *Hosea,* Hermemeia (series), Philadelphia, 1974

H. W. Wolff, *Joel and Amos,* Hermeneia, Philadelphia, 1977

J. L. Mays, *Amos,* OTL, London, 1969

J. H. Hayes, *Amos,* Nashville, 1988

H. W. Wolff, *Obadiah and Jonah,* Minneapolis, 1986

Jack M. Sasson, *Jonah,* AB, New York, 1990.

J. L. Mays, *Micah,* OTL, Philadelphia, 1976

D. R. Hillers, *Micah,* Hermeneia, Philadelphia, 1984

H. W. Wolff, *Micah,* Minneapolis, 1990

W. A Maier, *The Book of Nahum,* St. Louis, 1959

D. E. Gowan, *The Triumph of Faith in Habakkuk,* Atlanta, 1976

A. Kapelrud, *The Message of the Prophet Zephaniah,* Oslo, 1975

J. J. M. Roberts, *Nahum, Habakkuk, and Zephaniah,* OTL, Louisville, 1991

R. Mason, *The Books of Haggai, Zechariah, and Malachi,* Cambridge, 1977

D. E. Peterson, *Haggai and Zechariah 1-8,* OTL, Philadelphia, 1984

C. L. Meyers and E. M. Meyers, *Haggai, Zechariah 1-8,* AB, Garden City, 1987

Index

Index of Scriptural References

Jeremiah (Jer)